C000178920

SELECTED W

OLIVER GOLDSMITH was born in County Westmeath, Ireland, probably in 1729, the son of a curate. He was educated at Trinity College, Dublin and, after considering emigrating to America, went to Edinburgh in 1752 to study medicine. From 1754 to 1756 he travelled in Europe, eventually settling in London. He worked first as an assistant to an apothecary, then practised as a physician. He also began his career as a writer, and by 1757 was contributing articles to the *Monthly Review*. Although he remained impecunious, he was soon able to earn his living from his writing. The novel *The Vicar of Wakefield* (1766), the play *She Stoops to Conquer* (1773) and the narrative poem *The Deserted Village* (1770) brought him fame and success. By his death in 1774 Goldsmith was one of the best-known and most admired writers of his time.

JOHN LUCAS is Professor Emeritus of English at the universities of Loughborough and Nottingham Trent. Among his many critical and scholarly books are studies of Dickens, Elizabeth Gaskell and Arnold Bennett. He is the author of *England and Englishness: Poetry and Nationhood 1700–1900*, *Modern English Poetry: Hardy to Hughes*, and *The Radical Twenties*. John Lucas has also translated the poems of *Egil's Saga* and is the author of six collections of poetry, most recently *A World Perhaps: New and Selected Poems* (2002). Since 1994 he has been the publisher of Shoestring Press.

Fyfield*Books* aim to make available some of the great classics of British and European literature in clear, affordable formats, and to restore often neglected writers to their place in literary tradition.

Fyfield*Books* take their name from the Fyfield elm in Matthew Arnold's 'Scholar Gypsy' and 'Thyrsis'. The tree stood not far from the village where the series was originally devised in 1971.

> *Roam on! The light we sought is shining still.*
> *Dost thou ask proof? Our tree yet crowns the hill,*
> *Our Scholar travels yet the loved hill-side*

from 'Thyrsis'

OLIVER GOLDSMITH

Selected Writings

Edited with an introduction and afterword by
JOHN LUCAS

Fyfield*Books*

CARCANET

First published in Great Britain in 1988 by
Carcanet Press Limited
Alliance House
Cross Street
Manchester M2 7AQ

and

The Blackstaff Press Ltd
3 Galway Park
Dundonald
Belfast BT16 0AN

This impression 2003

Selection, introduction, afterword and editorial matter
© John Lucas 1988, 1990, 2003

The right of John Lucas to be identified as the editor of this work
has been asserted by him in accordance with the
Copyright, Designs and Patents Act of 1988
All rights reserved

A CIP catalogue record for this book is available from the British Library
ISBN 1 85754 703 9

The publisher acknowledges financial assistance from
the Arts Council of England

Printed and bound in England by SRP Ltd, Exeter

Contents

PROSE

Introduction

In 1753 Samuel Johnson, looking about him in search of an epithet that would make some sense of the times in which he lived, decided on 'an age of authors'. It may not be the definitive phrase to describe mid-eighteenth century England, but it has about it the ring of truth. For some decades previously, men of varying degrees of talent had been crowding into London, hoping to make their way in the city as writers. The recently established and rapidly expanding world of publishing provided numerous openings for 'scribblers', 'hacks', 'quill drivers': for all those who, dreaming of a career in this new industry, made up Grub Street. In fact, most scraped by. Some failed entirely. A few became famous. Among those shortly to arrive was Oliver Goldsmith.

Goldsmith's story is in many ways typical of the period. He had been born in County Westmeath, Ireland, most probably in 1729 (although there is some doubt about the actual year of his birth). Shortly afterwards his father became curate-in-charge of the parish of Kilkenny West and moved himself and his family to Lissoy, the village where Goldsmith spent most of his childhood. In 1745 he entered Trinity College, Dublin; having been reprimanded in 1747 for his part in a student riot, and awarded a degree in 1750, he took himself to County Roscommon (having failed to be ordained as a priest). Here he became a family tutor. But he soon tired of this work, shifted to Cork with the intention of emigrating to America, then turned back to Dublin. His family apparently offered to help finance law studies in London, but Goldsmith arrived instead in Edinburgh in 1752, to pursue the study of medicine. Two years later he left Edinburgh for Leyden, where he may or may not have continued his studies, but which he left in 1755 to travel erratically across Europe. His journeyings took him to Italy by way of France, Germany and Switzerland. In 1756 he arrived in London.

In her account of Goethe's Weimar, Marilyn Butler suggests that for the first time in Europe we have the spectacle of a highly educated middle-class male youth with little to occupy its attention. This distinction seems rather to belong to mid-eighteenth century England. Certainly, the London that Goldsmith settled into was awash with university 'wits' who found themselves without a career in prospect or the opportunity to make use of their education. Hence the dubious attractions of Grub Street. Not that Goldsmith immediately attempted to earn his living by his pen. At first he worked as an assistant to an apothecary and then as a physician in Southwark, although whether he was entitled to do this is uncertain, there being no evidence that he ever satisfactorily completed his medical studies. Nevertheless, it seems to have been at this time that he began to style himself Dr Oliver Goldsmith, and in 1758 he was offered the chance to become a civilian physician with the East India Company in Coromandel. To get there, however, he had to work his passage and the arrangements for this fell through. Goldsmith may not have been greatly worried by this apparent setback, for by now he was beginning to make his way as a writer.

The first evidence of his new career comes in 1757, when he began to contribute articles to the *Monthly Review*, one of the better-known and more prestigious journals of the time. Further commissions followed, other journals offered him work. The life of a literary hack began to take shape. In saying this I intend no slight. On the contrary, it is greatly to Goldsmith's credit that he could so successfully turn his hand to whatever his new masters required of him. He was by turns an essayist, a reviewer, a dramatist, a novelist, a librettist, a poet. By the time of his death, on 4 April 1774, he was among the best-known and most widely-admired writers of the age of authors. And yet it is obvious that like Johnson, whom he was to meet in 1761 and whose friend he became, Goldsmith is very much the writer-as-professional. As a result, he can on occasions be no more than a producer of consumables. Johnson remarked that nobody but a fool ever wrote anything except for money. He also and more famously noted that 'The Drama's Laws the Drama's Patrons give, / For we that live to please, must please to live.' Goldsmith, who was

8

frequently out of funds and often hounded by bailiffs, even after he had become well-enough known to be decently rewarded for his work, would have said amen to that. There is an almost cynical readiness to please about some of his writing. Perhaps this should not surprise us. The cynicism is, I think, the betraying evidence of what lurks beneath the pose which Goldsmith for the most part strikes very successfully, and which has much to do with the complications of his Anglo-Irishness, a matter I develop in my Afterword. Here, I will say only that while we need to register the cynicism, we nevertheless must be impressed by the scale of his achievement. For Goldsmith made a lasting contribution to every literary form he attempted; not even Johnson managed as much. The satiric essays that make up the *Citizen of the World* (1762), the novel *The Vicar of Wakefield* (1766), the play *She Stoops to Conquer* (1773), are all, deservedly, classics. And then there is the poetry, above all but by no means only, *The Deserted Village* (1770).

In his celebrated mock-epitaph on Goldsmith, David Garrick said that his friend 'wrote like an angel / But talk'd like Poor Poll'. This is often quoted with approval, and yet I am unhappy with its implications, no matter how generous the intention. Garrick's praise makes Goldsmith altogether too compliant, too sweet. It thus diverts attention away from sterner, more properly challenging qualities, to which we should pay attention. We will not, I admit, typically find them in the many songs and lighter pieces he wrote, which he published either separately or as part of longer works. Such works, of which 'An Elegy on the Death of a Mad Dog' may stand as example, are adroit, accomplished, polished – the exact words of praise spring readily enough to mind – but their counterparts exist in plenty among other poets of the period. And although the anapaestic tetrameters of 'The Haunch of Venison' and 'Retaliation' are managed with great verve, the metrical form inevitably limits what Goldsmith can say in these two 'sport' poems. The metre imposes its own conditions, makes for a special, reductive decorum. In these poems Goldsmith cannot help but come before us as a good-natured man.

9

In striking contrast, the couplets of 'The Traveller' and even more *The Deserted Village* require him to operate under no such constraint. For here a speaking voice comes into its own, deeply and subtly expressive. It is a voice which had been developed through the achievements of Goldsmith's great predecessors, especially Dryden and Pope, and I do not for a moment suggest that we are encouraged to think of it as personal. The 'I' of *The Deserted Village* is not individualised in any important way. It is offered as representative of generous outrage, of long-considered political and social ideas, of human/humane convictions: it is, in short, the voice of the model citizen, speaking to its audience and on that audience's behalf. The greatness of *The Deserted Village* has much to do with Goldsmith's ability to make us feel that what is being said is in no sense contentious. And yet what he is doing is, of course, contentious in the extreme. For as my Afterword explains, Goldsmith's politics are far more questioning and finally radical than commentators have been willing to acknowledge. Moreover, in *The Deserted Village* he takes over a genre, or perhaps sub-genre, the pastoral-as-picturesque, and makes of it something new and valuable. This deserves some comment.

It is of the nature of pastoral poetry to be politically and socially conservative. This is not to say that it cannot be used in other ways and towards other ends, but for the most part such poetry produces accounts of relationships within a rural context that endorses stability. 'Harmony' is what pastoral celebrates: harmony between man and nature and between man and man (and, occasionally, women). William Empson long ago pointed out how the idea of stability operates as the ground-politics of Gray's 'Elegy Written in a Country Churchyard'. Commenting on the famous stanza where Gray writes of the flower 'born to blush unseen / And waste its sweetness on the desert air', Empson remarked that it is all one to the flower whether it is seen or no. By implication, therefore, those who dwell in the 'cool, sequestered vale of life' are content to stay there. Gray's 'Elegy' is the greatest of a vast number of eighteenth-century poems which speak in praise of 'retirement', of the untroubled tranquillity of rural life; and which frequently adopt a mode of narration and poetic form that distance the rural scene evoked. The ballad, the Spenserian stanza form, tamed Miltonics: these are a few of the framing devices by means of which poets create works which are, then, bound to glow with nostalgia. Such a glow may seem to hang about Goldsmith's Auburn. But his unsurprising couplets and the voice in which they are uttered make *The Deserted Village* a contemporary poem, one that is insistently engaged in present realities. In other words, it is not meant to be an 'original' poem, a novelty, a 'sport'. And by implication it criticises those many poems that refused to be seriously engaged with the issues that 'pastoralism' was used to evade. To say this brings me to the picturesque.

Briefly, the cult of the picturesque was one of those expressions of tiresome and sterile aesthetics that play a major and debilitating role in the development of eighteenth-century taste. It was essentially for the cultivated town-dweller, who was encouraged to find art in nature by considering how nature could often look like, or be made to look like, the kinds of ideal landscapes that had become tyrannously familiar through the much-praised and widely-imitated work of the seventeenth-century French painter, Claude Lorraine. A picturesque landscape was required – and chosen – to look like a picturesque painting (and the effects of the famous Claude glass could be used to heighten the similarities). The appropriate landscape would include certain constituent elements; and as Martin Price has said in his excellent essay, 'The Picturesque Moment', its aesthetic lay 'in the emergence of formal interest from an unlikely source (the hovel, the gypsy, the ass), or in the internal conflict between the centrifugal forces of dissolution and centripetal pull of form (ruined temples, aged men).' Picturesque landscapes were supposed to inspire a feeling of pleasing melancholy: you looked and you mused on the grandeur of nature and the impermanence of man (hence the ruins and aged characters). The picturesque took for granted 'the principle of change'.

11

Even from this brief account it should be possible to see why the level, civilised anger of Goldsmith's poem is partly directed against the aestheticism of the picturesque. At first glance, *The Deserted Village* takes up and offers to comment on a purely picturesque subject. It seems to be about the principle of change, the ruins of time; it even has an old 'picturesque' woman wandering about the decayed village. But what is so challenging about the poem is Goldsmith's insistence on our recognising that change has occurred not through some 'principle' but through actual human agency, through 'the tyrant's hand', through the work of 'One only master'. In short, Goldsmith is writing about enclosure, in this instance for emparkment, which then becomes the evidence of an entirely selfish leisure which wrecks the purposive lives of others.

It is often remarked that 'Auburn' is generalised to such an extent that it is impossible to track down a 'real life' counterpart. Was it Lissoy, was it Nuneham Courtenay? Not being able to tell, some critics have felt that Goldsmith has produced an unacceptable 'mythic' village. It is certainly true that the poem finds for each detail of the village the appropriate and, as it may seem, generalising epithet:

> The sheltered cot, the cultivated farm,
> The never-failing brook, the busy mill,
> The decent church that topped the neighbouring hill,
> The hawthorn bush, with seats beneath the shade,
> For talking age and whispering lovers made.

Here, even the alliterations seem to help us bind up the account of village life into one of great sweetness and harmony. But if this is to write like an angel, it is also to write with real seriousness of purpose. For this image of harmonious content is then shown to be helplessly vulnerable, so that those who cherish the pastoral as a literary form, as something for purely aesthetic consideration, are made to consider what *actually* happens in rural relations; and those who go in search of the picturesque are made to consider how ruins *actually* come about. The result is that by the time

12

Goldsmith comes to speak of the man of wealth and pride, and to note that 'The robe that wraps his limbs in silken sloth / Has robbed the neighbouring fields of half their growth', the connections between wealth and despoliation have been so thoroughly pointed up that the political mystifications of pastoral and picturesque cannot be sustained. Moreover, Goldsmith's uniquely brilliant use of the transferred epithet (a matter about which Donald Davie wrote definitively in *Purity of Diction in English Verse*), is functionally exact. Here, it shows in the way he moves 'silken' from the word 'robe', where it most obviously belongs, to 'sloth'. The tactic enables us both to savour the imaginative wit that connects by sound the words 'silken' and 'sloth' and, more importantly, to register how Goldsmith identifies the man of pride's 'sloth' with a social ease, a silky assurance, so as to point up his assumption that he is 'naturally' entitled to ruin other people's lives. And this then makes it possible for us to recognize that the person who speaks the poem has his own assurance – call it poise – that is truly civilized in so far as it makes plain how and why his allegiances are produced, how and why his indignation is directed towards those who presume to identify with 'the gloss of art'. In short, the poem's often astringent wit is inseparable from a readiness to bear witness which amounts to true integrity of judgement, political, social, moral, cultural. If an age of authors can mean an age of time-servers, the importance of *The Deserted Village* is that it restores to authorship its proper authority.

And this is generally true of Goldsmith's best work. The wit, the civility of tone, the adroit handling of form: these are all at the service of something essentially serious, they embody qualities which I would call 'citizenship'. For this word alerts us to Goldsmith's concern that the society from which he writes and which he addresses is, increasingly, breaking up into private, competing, and ultimately de-humanising interests and forces, which it is the requirement of his poetry to oppose. And it then follows that he is, or ought to be, required reading.

13

A Note on the Texts

For the poems I have leaned heavily on Roger Lonsdale's splendid edition of *The Poems of Gray, Collins and Goldsmith*, Longmans, 1969. I have also consulted the 2-volume *Poetical and Dramatic Works of Oliver Goldsmith M.B.* printed by T. Goldney, for Messieurs Rivington, T. Carnan, E. Newbery, and T. Nicholl, London, 1786, and Gilfillan's edition of *The Poetical Works of Goldsmith, Collins and T. Warton*, the text edited by Charles Cowden Clarke, Edinburgh and London, 1863.

For the prose I have gone most frequently to the *Collected Works of Oliver Goldsmith*, 5 volumes, ed. Arthur Friedman, Oxford, 1966; and I have also made use of Richard Garnett's excellent *Goldsmith: Selected Works*, Rupert Hart-Davis, 1950 (The Reynard Library). *The Collected Letters* are edited by Katharine C. Balderston, Cambridge, 1928.

In the poetry and prose I have occasionally silently emended both spelling and punctuation, in order to bring them into line with modern usage, where this can be done without affecting meaning.

Both poems and prose appear in chronological order of composition (where this can be determined) or of publication. Since Goldsmith wrote for a living, much that he produced was written to order, but through most of it his own preoccupations gleam, and I have tried to select in such a way as to suggest where the gleams are brightest.

A Prologue,

written and spoken by the poet Laberius, a Roman knight, whom Cæsar
forced upon the stage.
(preserved by Macrobius).

What! no way left to shun the inglorious stage,
And save from infamy my sinking age!
Scarce half alive, oppressed with many a year,
What in the name of dotage drives me here?
A time there was, when glory was my guide,
Nor force nor fraud could turn my steps aside;
Unawed by power, and unappalled by fear,
With honest thrift I held my honour dear;
But this vile hour disperses all my store,
And all my hoard of honour is no more.
For ah! too partial to my life's decline,
Cæsar persuades, submission must be mine;
Him I obey, whom Heaven itself obeys,
Hopeless of pleasing, yet inclined to please.
Here then at once I welcome every shame,
And cancel at three-score a life of fame;
No more my titles shall my children tell,
"The old buffoon" will fit my name as well;
This day beyond its term my fate extends,
For life is ended when our honour ends.

On a Beautiful Youth Struck Blind with Lightning
(imitated from the Spanish)

Sure 'twas by Providence designed,
Rather in pity than in hate,
That he should be like Cupid blind,
To save him from Narcissus' fate.

15

The Gift
To Iris, in Bow Street, Covent Garden

Say, cruel Iris, pretty rake,
   Dear mercenary beauty,
What annual offering shall I make,
   Expressive of my duty?

My heart, a victim to thine eyes,
   Should I at once deliver,
Say, would the angry fair one prize
   The gift, who slights the giver?

A bill, a jewel, watch, or toy,
   My rivals give – and let 'em:
If gems or gold impart a joy,
   I'll give them – when I get 'em.

I'll give – but not the full-blown rose,
   Or rosebud more in fashion;
Such short-lived offerings but disclose
   A transitory passion.

I'll give thee something yet unpaid,
   Not less sincere than civil:
I'll give thee – ah! too charming maid,
   I'll give thee – to the devil.

A Sonnet

Weeping, murmuring, complaining,
   Lost to every gay delight,
Myra, too sincere for feigning,
   Fears the approaching bridal night.

16

Yet why impair thy bright perfection,
    Or dim thy beauty with a tear?
Had Myra followed my direction,
    She long had wanted cause of fear.

An Elegy on the Glory of Her Sex, Mrs Mary Blaize

Good people all, with one accord,
    Lament for Madam Blaize,
Who never wanted a good word –
    From those who spoke her praise.

The needy seldom passed her door,
    And always found her kind:
She freely lent to all the poor –
    Who left a pledge behind.

She strove the neighbourhood to please,
    With manners wondrous winning;
And never followed wicked ways –
    Unless when she was sinning.

At church, in silks and satins new,
    With hoop of monstrous size;
She never slumbered in her pew –
    But when she shut her eyes.

Her love was sought, I do aver,
    By twenty beaux and more;
The king himself has followed her –
    When she has walked before.

17

But now her wealth and finery fled,
  Her hangers-on cut short all:
The doctors found, when she was dead –
  Her last disorder mortal.

Let us lament, in sorrow sore,
  For Kent Street well may say,
That, had she lived a twelvemonth more –
  She had not died to-day.

The Double Transformation
A Tale

Secluded from domestic strife,
Jack Bookworm led a college life;
A fellowship at twenty-five,
Made him the happiest man alive;
He drank his glass, and cracked his joke,
And freshmen wondered as he spoke.
  Such pleasures, unalloyed with care,
Could any accident impair?
Could Cupid's shaft at length transfix
Our swain, arrived at thirty-six?
Oh! had the archer ne'er come down
To ravage in a country town,
Or Flavia been content to stop
At triumphs in a Fleet Street shop:
Oh! had her eyes forgot to blaze,
Or Jack had wanted eyes to gaze!
Oh! – But let exclamation cease,
Her presence banished all his peace:
So with decorum all things carried,
Miss frowned, and blushed, and then was – married.

18

Need we expose to vulgar sight
The raptures of the bridal night?
Need we intrude on hallowed ground,
Or draw the curtains closed around?
Let it suffice, that each had charms:
He clasped a goddess in his arms;
And though she felt his visage rough,
Yet in a man 'twas well enough.

   The honey-moon like lightning flew;
The second brought its transports too;
A third, a fourth, were not amiss;
The fifth was friendship mixed with bliss:
But when a twelvemonth passed away,
Jack found his goddess made of clay;
Found half the charms that decked her face
Arose from powder, shreds, or lace:
But still the worst remained behind,
That very face had robbed her mind.

   Skilled in no other arts was she,
But dressing, patching, repartee;
And, just as humour rose or fell,
By turns a slattern or a belle;
'Tis true she dressed with modern grace,
Half naked at a ball or race;
But when at home, at board or bed,
Five greasy nightcaps wrapped her head.
Could so much beauty condescend
To be a dull domestic friend?
Could any curtain lectures bring
To decency so fine a thing?
In short, by night, 'twas fits or fretting;
By day, 'twas gadding or coquetting.
Fond to be seen, she kept a bevy
Of powdered coxcombs at her levee:
The squire and captain too their stations,
And twenty other near relations:

Jack sucked his pipe and often broke
A sigh in suffocating smoke;
While all their hours were passed between
Insulting repartee or spleen.

Thus as her faults each day were known,
He thinks her features coarser grown;
He fancies every vice she shows,
Or thins her lip or points her nose:
Whenever rage or envy rise,
How wide her mouth, how wild her eyes!
He knows not how, but so it is,
Her face is grown a knowing phiz;
And, though her fops are wondrous civil,
He thinks her ugly as the devil.

Now, to perplex the ravelled noose,
As each a different way pursues,
While sullen or loquacious strife
Promised to hold them on for life,
That dire disease, whose ruthless power
Withers the beauty's transient flower,
Lo! the small-pox, with horrid glare
Levelled its terrors at the fair;
And, rifling every youthful grace,
Left but the remnant of a face.

The glass, grown hateful to her sight,
Reflected now a perfect fright;
Each former art she vainly tries
To bring back lustre to her eyes.
In vain she tries her pastes and creams,
To smooth her skin, or hide its seams;
Her country beaux and city cousins,
Lovers no more, flew off by dozens;
The squire himself was seen to yield,
And even the captain quit the field.

Poor madam, now condemned to hack
The rest of life with anxious Jack,

Perceiving others fairly flown,
Attempted pleasing him alone.
Jack soon was dazzled to behold
Her present face surpass the old;
With modesty her cheeks are dyed,
Humility displaces pride;
For tawdry finery is seen
A person ever neatly clean;
No more presuming on her sway,
She learns good-nature every day:
Serenely gay, and strict in duty,
Jack finds his wife a perfect beauty.

Description of an Author's Bed-chamber

Where the Red Lion, flaring o'er the way,
Invites each passing stranger that can pay;
Where Calvert's butt, and Parson's black champagne,
Regale the drabs and bloods of Drury Lane;
There in a lonely room, from bailiffs snug,
The Muse found Scroggen stretched beneath a rug.
A window patched with paper lent a ray,
That dimly showed the state in which he lay;
The sanded floor that grits beneath the tread,
The humid wall with paltry pictures spread;
The royal game of goose was there in view,
And the twelve rules the royal martyr drew;
The Seasons framed with listing found a place,
And brave Prince William showed his lamp-black face:
The morn was cold, he views with keen desire
The rusty grate unconscious of a fire;

With beer and milk arrears the frieze was scored,
And five cracked tea-cups dressed the chimney board;
A nightcap decked his brows instead of bay,
A cap by night – a stocking all the day!

On Seeing Mrs *** Perform in the Character of ***

To you, bright fair, the nine address their lays,
And tune my feeble voice to sing thy praise.
The heartfelt power of every charm divine,
Who can withstand their all-commanding shine?
See how she moves along with every grace,
While soul-brought tears steal down each shining face.
She speaks, 'tis rapture all and nameless bliss;
Ye gods, what transport e'er compared to this.
As when in Paphian groves the Queen of Love
With fond complaint addressed the listening Jove,
'Twas joy and endless blisses all around,
And rocks forgot their hardness at the sound.
Then first, at last even Jove was taken in,
And felt her charms, without disguise, within.

On the Death of the Right Honourable ***

Ye Muses, pour the pitying tear
For Pollio snatched away;
Oh had he lived another year!
He had not died today.

Oh, were he born to bless mankind,
In virtuous times of yore,
Heroes themselves had fallen behind!
When'er he went before.

How sad the groves and plains appear,
And sympathetic sheep;
Even pitying hills would drop a tear!
If hills could learn to weep.

His bounty in exalted strain
Each bard might well display;
Since none implored relief in vain!
That went relieved away.

And hark! I hear the tuneful throng
His obsequies forbid.
He still shall live, shall live as long!
As ever dead man did.

An Elegy on the Death of a Mad Dog

Good people all, of every sort,
   Give ear unto my song;
And if you find it wondrous short,
   It cannot hold you long.

In Islington there was a man,
   Of whom the world might say,
That still a godly race he ran,
   Whene'er he went to pray.

23

A kind and gentle heart he had,
    To comfort friends and foes;
The naked every day he clad,
    When he put on his clothes.

And in that town a dog was found,
    As many dogs there be,
Both mongrel, puppy, whelp, and hound,
    And curs of low degree.

This dog and man at first were friends;
    But when a pique began,
The dog, to gain some private ends,
    Went mad and bit the man.

Around from all the neighbouring streets
    The wondering neighbours ran,
And swore the dog had lost his wits,
    To bite so good a man.

The wound it seemed both sore and sad
    To every Christian eye;
And while they swore the dog was mad,
    They swore the man would die.

But soon a wonder came to light,
    That showed the rogues they lied;
The man recovered of the bite,
    The dog it was that died.

Stanzas on Woman

When lovely woman stoops to folly,
  And finds too late that men betray,
What charm can soothe her melancholy,
  What art can wash her guilt away?

The only art her guilt to cover,
  To hide her shame from every eye,
To give repentance to her lover,
And wring his bosom – is, to die.

Edwin and Angelina

"Turn, gentle Hermit of the dale,
  And guide my lonely way,
To where yon taper cheers the vale
  With hospitable ray.

"For here forlorn and lost I tread,
  With fainting steps and slow;
Where wilds immeasurably spread,
  Seem lengthening as I go."

"Forbear, my son," the Hermit cries,
  "To tempt the dangerous gloom;
For yonder faithless phantom flies
  To lure thee to thy doom.

"Here to the houseless child of want
  My door is open still;
And though my portion is but scant,
  I give it with good will.

25

"Then turn to-night, and freely share
  Whate'er my cell bestows;
My rushy couch and frugal fare,
  My blessing and repose.

"No flocks that range the valley free
  To slaughter I condemn;
Taught by that Power that pities me,
  I learn to pity them.

"But from the mountain's grassy side
  A guiltless feast I bring;
A scrip with herbs and fruits supplied,
  And water from the spring.

"Then, pilgrim, turn, thy cares forego;
  All earth-born cares are wrong;
Man wants but little here below,
  Nor wants that little long."

Soft as the dew from heaven descends,
  His gentle accents fell:
The modest stranger lowly bends,
  And follows to the cell.

Far in a wilderness obscure
  The lonely mansion lay;
A refuge to the neighbouring poor,
  And strangers led astray.

No stores beneath its humble thatch
  Required a master's care;
The wicket, opening with a latch,
  Received the harmless pair.

And now, when busy crowds retire
    To take their evening rest,
The Hermit trimmed his little fire,
    And cheered his pensive guest:

And spread his vegetable store,
    And gaily prest, and smiled;
And, skilled in legendary lore,
    The lingering hours beguiled.

Around in sympathetic mirth
    Its tricks the kitten tries;
The cricket chirrups in the hearth;
    The crackling faggot flies.

But nothing could a charm impart,
    To soothe the stranger's woe;
For grief was heavy at his heart,
    And tears began to flow.

His rising cares the Hermit spied,
    With answering care opprest:
And, "Whence, unhappy youth," he cried,
    "The sorrows of thy breast?

"From better habitations spurned,
    Reluctant dost thou rove?
Or grieve for friendship unreturned,
    Or unregarded love?

"Alas! the joys that fortune brings
    Are trifling, and decay;
And those who prize the paltry things,
    More trifling still than they.

"And what is friendship but a name,
    A charm that lulls to sleep;
A shade that follows wealth or fame,
    But leaves the wretch to weep?

"And love is still an emptier sound,
    The modern fair one's jest;
On earth unseen, or only found
    To warm the turtle's nest.

"For shame, fond youth! thy sorrows hush,
    And spurn the sex," he said:
But while he spoke, a rising blush
    His love-lorn guest betrayed.

Surprised, he sees new beauties rise,
    Swift mantling to the view;
Like colours o'er the morning skies,
    As bright, as transient too.

The bashful look, the rising breast,
    Alternate spread alarms:
The lovely stranger stands confest
    A maid in all her charms.

And, "Ah! forgive a stranger rude,
    A wretch forlorn," she cried;
"Whose feet unhallowed thus intrude
    Where heaven and you reside.

"But let a maid thy pity share,
    Whom love has taught to stray;
Who seeks for rest, but finds despair
    Companion of her way.

"My father lived beside the Tyne,
   A wealthy lord was he;
And all his wealth was marked as mine,
   He had but only me.

"To win me from his tender arms,
   Unnumbered suitors came;
Who praised me for imputed charms,
   And felt, or feigned, a flame.

"Each hour a mercenary crowd
   With richest proffers strove;
Among the rest, young Edwin bowed,
   But never talked of love.

"In humble, simplest habit clad,
   No wealth nor power had he;
Wisdom and worth were all he had,
   But these were all to me.

"And when, beside me in the dale,
   He carolled lays of love;
His breath lent fragrance to the gale,
   And music to the grove.

"The blossom opening to the day,
   The dews of heaven refined,
Could naught of purity display,
   To emulate his mind.

"The dew, the blossoms of the tree,
   With charms inconstant shine:
Their charms were his, but, woe to me!
   Their constancy was mine.

"For still I tried each fickle art,
    Importunate and vain;
And, while his passion touched my heart,
    I triumphed in his pain.

"Till quite dejected with my scorn,
    He left me to my pride;
And sought a solitude forlorn,
    In secret, where he died.

"But mine the sorrow, mine the fault,
    And well my life shall pay;
I'll seek the solitude he sought,
    And stretch me where he lay.

"And there forlorn, despairing, hid,
    I'll lay me down and die;
'Twas so for me that Edwin did,
    And so for him will I."

"Forbid it, Heaven!" the Hermit cried,
    And clasped her to his breast:
The wondering fair one turned to chide, –
    'Twas Edwin's self that pressed!

"Turn, Angelina, ever dear,
    My charmer, turn to see
Thy own, thy long-lost Edwin here,
    Restored to love and thee.

"Thus let me hold thee to my heart,
    And every care resign:
And shall we never, never part,
    My life – my all that's mine?

"No, never from this hour to part,
    We'll live and love so true;
The sigh that rends thy constant heart
    Shall break thy Edwin's too."

Songs
from the oratorio of "The Captivity"

The wretch, condemned with life to part,
    Still, still on hope relies;
And every pang that rends the heart
    Bids expectation rise.

Hope, like the glimmering taper's light,
    Adorns and cheers the way;
And still, as darker grows the night,
    Emits a brighter ray.

O Memory, thou fond deceiver,
    Still importunate and vain,
To former joys recurring ever,
    And turning all the past to pain!

Thou, like the world, the opprest oppressing,
    Thy smiles increase the wretch's woe;
And he who wants each other blessing,
    In thee must ever find a foe.

31

The Traveller
or, a Prospect of Society

Remote, unfriended, melancholy, slow,
Or by the lazy Scheldt or wandering Po;
Or onward, where the rude Carinthian boor
Against the houseless stranger shuts the door;
Or where Campania's plain forsaken lies,
A weary waste expanding to the skies;
Where'er I roam, whatever realms to see,
My heart untravelled fondly turns to thee:
Still to my brother turns, with ceaseless pain,
And drags at each remove a lengthening chain.   10

    Eternal blessings crown my earliest friend,
And round his dwelling guardian saints attend;
Blest be that spot, where cheerful guests retire
To pause from toil, and trim their evening fire:
Blest that abode, where want and pain repair,
And every stranger finds a ready chair:
Blest be those feasts with simple plenty crowned,
Where all the ruddy family around
Laugh at the jests or pranks that never fail,
Or sigh with pity at some mournful tale;   20
Or press the bashful stranger to his food,
And learn the luxury of doing good.

    But me, not destined such delights to share,
My prime of life in wandering spent and care;
Impelled with steps unceasing to pursue
Some fleeting good, that mocks me with the view;
That, like the circle bounding earth and skies,
Allures from far, yet, as I follow, flies;
My fortune leads to traverse realms alone,
And find no spot of all the world my own.   30

    Even now, where Alpine solitudes ascend,
I sit me down a pensive hour to spend;
And, placed on high above the storm's career,

Look downward where a hundred realms appear:
Lakes, forests, cities, plains extending wide,
The pomp of kings, the shepherd's humbler pride.
　　When thus Creation's charms around combine,
Amidst the store should thankless pride repine?
Say, should the philosophic mind disdain
That good which makes each humbler bosom vain? 40
Let school-taught pride dissemble all it can,
These little things are great to little man;
And wiser he, whose sympathetic mind
Exults in all the good of all mankind.
Ye glittering towns, with wealth and splendour crowned;
Ye fields, where summer spreads profusion round;
Ye lakes, whose vessels catch the busy gale;
Ye bending swains, that dress the flowery vale;
For me your tributary stores combine:
Creation's heir, the world, the world is mine. 50
　　As some lone miser, visiting his store,
Bends at his treasure, counts, recounts it o'er;
Hoards after hoards his rising raptures fill,
Yet still he sighs, for hoards are wanting still:
Thus to my breast alternate passions rise,
Pleased with each good that Heaven to man supplies:
Yet oft a sigh prevails, and sorrows fall,
To see the hoard of human bliss so small;
And oft I wish amidst the scene to find
Some spot to real happiness consigned, 60
Where my worn soul, each wandering hope at rest,
May gather bliss to see my fellows blest.
　　But where to find that happiest spot below,
Who can direct, when all pretend to know?
The shuddering tenant of the frigid zone
Boldly proclaims that happiest spot his own;
Extols the treasures of his stormy seas,
And his long nights of revelry and ease:
The naked Negro, panting at the line,

33

Boasts of his golden sands and palmy wine, 70
Basks in the glare, or stems the tepid wave,
And thanks his gods for all the good they gave.
Such is the patriot's boast, where'er we roam,
His first, best country, ever is at home.
And yet, perhaps, if countries we compare,
And estimate the blessings which they share,
Though patriots flatter, still shall wisdom find
An equal portion dealt to all mankind,
As different good, by Art or Nature given,
To different nations, makes their blessings even. 80
    Nature, a mother kind alike to all,
Still grants her bliss at labour's earnest call;
With food as well the peasant is supplied
On Idra's cliff as Arno's shelvy side;
And though the rocky-crested summits frown,
These rocks, by custom, turn to beds of down.
From Art more various are the blessings sent;
Wealth, commerce, honour, liberty, content:
Yet these each other's power so strong contest,
That either seems destructive of the rest. 90
Where wealth and freedom reign, contentment fails,
And honour sinks where commerce long prevails.
Hence every state, to one loved blessing prone,
Conforms and models life to that alone:
Each to the favourite happiness attends,
And spurns the plan that aims at other ends;
Till, carried to excess in each domain,
This favourite good begets peculiar pain.
    But let us try these truths with closer eyes,
And trace them through the prospect as it lies: 100
Here for a while, my proper cares resigned,
Here let me sit in sorrow for mankind;
Like yon neglected shrub at random cast,
That shades the steep and sighs at every blast.
    Far to the right, where Apennine ascends,

Bright as the summer, Italy extends;
Its uplands sloping deck the mountain's side,
Woods over woods in gay theatric pride;
While oft some temple's mouldering tops between,
With venerable grandeur mark the scene.   110
　　Could Nature's bounty satisfy the breast,
The sons of Italy were surely blest.
Whatever fruits in different climes are found,
That proudly rise, or humbly court the ground;
Whatever blooms in torrid tracts appear,
Whose bright succession decks the varied year;
Whatever sweets salute the northern sky
With vernal lives that blossom but to die:
These here disporting own the kindred soil,
Nor ask luxuriance from the planter's toil;   120
While sea-born gales their gelid wings expand,
To winnow fragrance round the smiling land.
　　But small the bliss that sense alone bestows,
And sensual bliss is all the nation knows.
In florid beauty groves and fields appear;
Man seems the only growth that dwindles here,
Contrasted faults through all his manners reign;
Though poor, luxurious; though submissive, vain;
Though grave, yet trifling; zealous, yet untrue;
And even in penance planning sins anew.   130
All evils here contaminate the mind,
That opulence departed leaves behind;
For wealth was theirs; nor far removed the date,
When Commerce proudly flourished through the state:
At her command the palace learnt to rise;
Again the long-fallen column sought the skies;
The canvas glowed, beyond even Nature warm,
The pregnant quarry teemed with human form;
Till, more unsteady than the southern gale,
Commerce on other shores displayed her sail;   140
While naught remained of all that riches gave,

35

But towns unmanned and lords without a slave;
And late the nation found, with fruitless skill,
Its former strength was but plethoric ill.
  Yet still the loss of wealth is here supplied
By arts, the splendid wrecks of former pride;
From these the feeble heart and long-fallen mind
An easy compensation seem to find.
Here may be seen, in bloodless pomp arrayed,
The pasteboard triumph and the cavalcade;   150
Processions formed for piety and love,
A mistress or a saint in every grove.
By sports like these are all their cares beguiled;
The sports of children satisfy the child:
Each nobler aim, repressed by long control,
Now sinks at last or feebly mans the soul;
While low delights succeeding fast behind,
In happier meanness occupy the mind:
As in those domes where Cæsars once bore sway,
Defaced by time and tottering in decay,   160
There in the ruin, heedless of the dead,
The shelter-seeking peasant builds his shed,
And, wondering man could want the larger pile,
Exults, and owns his cottage with a smile.
  My soul, turn from them, turn we to survey
Where rougher climes a nobler race display,
Where the bleak Swiss their stormy mansions tread,
And force a churlish soil for scanty bread.
No product here the barren hills afford,
But man and steel, the soldier and his sword;   170
No vernal blooms their torpid rocks array,
But winter lingering chills the lap of May;
No zephyr fondly sues the mountain's breast,
But meteors glare and stormy glooms invest.
  Yet still, even here, content can spread a charm,
Redress the clime and all its rage disarm.
Though poor the peasant's hut, his feasts though small,

He sees his little lot the lot of all;
Sees no contiguous palace rear its head,
To shame the meanness of his humble shed;   180
No costly lord the sumptuous banquet deal
To make him loathe his vegetable meal:
But calm, and bred in ignorance and toil,
Each wish contracting fits him to the soil:
Cheerful at morn he wakes from short repose,
Breathes the keen air and carols as he goes;
With patient angle trolls the finny deep,
Or drives his venturous ploughshare to the steep;
Or seeks the den where snow-tracks mark the way,
And drags the struggling savage into day.   190
At night returning, every labour sped,
He sits him down, the monarch of a shed;
Smiles by his cheerful fire, and round surveys
His children's looks, that brighten at the blaze;
While his loved partner, boastful of her hoard,
Displays her cleanly platter on the board:
And haply too some pilgrim, thither led,
With many a tale repays the nightly bed.
   Thus every good his native wilds impart,
Imprints the patriot passion on his heart;   200
And even those hills, that round his mansion rise,
Enhance the bliss his scanty fund supplies.
Dear is that shed to which his soul conforms,
And dear that hill which lifts him to the storms;
And as a child, when scaring sounds molest,
Clings close and closer to the mother's breast,
So the loud torrent and the whirlwind's roar
But bind him to his native mountains more.
   Such are the charms to barren states assigned;
Their wants but few, their wishes all confined: 210
Yet let them only share the praises due;
If few their wants, their pleasures are but few:
For every want that stimulates the breast

Becomes a source of pleasure when redrest:
Whence from such lands each pleasing science flies,
That first excites desire, and then supplies;
Unknown to them, when sensual pleasures cloy,
To fill the languid pause with finer joy;
Unknown those powers that raise the soul to flame,
Catch every nerve and vibrate through the frame.   220
Their level life is but a mouldering fire,
Unquenched by want, unfanned by strong desire;
Unfit for raptures, or, if raptures cheer
On some high festival of once a year,
In wild excess the vulgar breast takes fire,
Till, buried in debauch, the bliss expire.
    But not their joys alone thus coarsely flow;
Their morals, like their pleasures, are but low;
For, as refinement stops, from sire to son
Unaltered, unimproved the manners run;   230
And love's and friendship's finely-pointed dart
Falls blunted from each indurated heart.
Some sterner virtues o'er the mountain's breast
May sit, like falcons cowering on the nest;
But all the gentler morals, such as play
Through life's more cultured walks, and charm the way,
These, far dispersed, on timorous pinions fly,
To sport and flutter in a kinder sky.
    To kinder skies, where gentler manners reign,
I turn; and France displays her bright domain.   240
Gay, sprightly land of mirth and social ease,
Pleased with thyself, whom all the world can please,
How often have I led thy sportive choir,
With tuneless pipe, beside the murmuring Loire.
Where shading elms along the margin grew,
And freshened from the wave the zephyr flew:
And haply, though my harsh touch faltering still
But mocked all tune and marred the dancer's skill,
Yet would the village praise my wondrous power,

And dance, forgetful of the noontide hour. 250
Alike all ages: dames of ancient days
Have led their children through the mirthful maze;
And the gay grandsire, skilled in gestic lore,
Has frisked beneath the burden of threescore.
  So blest a life these thoughtless realms display;
Thus idly busy rolls their world away.
Theirs are those arts that mind to mind endear,
For honour forms the social temper here:
Honour, that praise which real merit gains,
Or even imaginary worth obtains, 260
Here passes current; paid from hand to hand,
It shifts in splendid traffic round the land:
From courts to camps, to cottages it strays,
And all are taught an avarice of praise;
They please, are pleased; they give to get esteem,
Till, seeming blest, they grow to what they seem.
  But while this softer art their bliss supplies.
It gives their follies also room to rise;
For praise too dearly loved, or warmly sought,
Enfeebles all internal strength of thought; 270
And the weak soul, within itself unblest,
Leans for all pleasure on another's breast.
Hence Ostentation here, with tawdry art,
Pants for the vulgar praise which fools impart;
Here Vanity assumes her pert grimace,
And trims her robes of frieze with copper lace;
Here beggar Pride defrauds her daily cheer,
To boast one splendid banquet once a year;
The mind still turns where shifting fashion draws,
Nor weighs the solid worth of self-applause. 280
  To men of other minds my fancy flies,
Embosomed in the deep where Holland lies.
Methinks her patient sons before me stand,
Where the broad ocean leans against the land,
And, sedulous to stop the coming tide,

39

Lift the tall rampire's artificial pride.
Onward, methinks, and diligently slow,
The firm connected bulwark seems to grow;
Spreads its long arms amidst the watery roar,
Scoops out an empire, and usurps the shore: 290
While the pent ocean, rising o'er the pile,
Sees an amphibious world beneath him smile;
The slow canal, the yellow-blossomed vale,
The willow-tufted bank, the gliding sail,
The crowded mart, the cultivated plain,
A new creation rescued from his reign.
    Thus, while around the wave-subjected soil
Impels the native to repeated toil,
Industrious habits in each bosom reign,
And industry begets a love of gain.   300
Hence all the good from opulence that springs,
With all those ills superfluous treasure brings,
Are here displayed. Their much-loved wealth imparts
Convenience, plenty, elegance and arts;
But view them closer, craft and fraud appear,
Even liberty itself is bartered here.
At gold's superior charms all freedom flies,
The needy sell it, and the rich man buys;
A land of tyrants, and a den of slaves,
Here wretches seek dishonourable graves,   310
And calmly bent, to servitude conform,
Dull as their lakes that slumber in the storm.
    Heavens! how unlike their Belgic sires of old!
Rough, poor, content, ungovernably bold;
War in each breast, and freedom on each brow:
How much unlike the sons of Britain now!
    Fired at the sound, my genius spreads her wing,
And flies where Britain courts the western spring;
Where lawns extend that scorn Arcadian pride,
And brighter streams than famed Hydaspes glide.   320
There all around the gentlest breezes stray,

There gentle music melts on every spray;
Creation's mildest charms are there combined,
Extremes are only in the master's mind;
Stern o'er each bosom Reason holds her state,
With daring aims irregularly great:
Pride in their port, defiance in their eye,
I see the lords of human kind pass by,
Intent on high designs, a thoughtful band,
By forms unfashioned, fresh from Nature's hand;   330
Fierce in their native hardiness of soul,
True to imagined right, above control,
While even the peasant boasts these rights to scan,
And learns to venerate himself as man.

Thine, Freedom, thine the blessings pictured here,
Thine are those charms that dazzle and endear;
Too blest indeed, were such without alloy,
But fostered even by Freedom, ills annoy;
That independence Britons prize too high,
Keeps man from man, and breaks the social tie;   340
The self-depended lordlings stand alone,
All claims that bind and sweeten life unknown;
Here, by the bonds of nature feebly held,
Minds combat minds, repelling and repelled;
Ferments arise, imprisoned factions roar,
Repressed ambition struggles round her shore,
Till over-wrought, the general system feels
Its motions stopped or frenzy fire the wheels.

Nor this the worst. As nature's ties decay,
As duty, love and honour fail to sway,   350
Fictitious bonds, the bonds of wealth and law,
Still gather strength, and force unwilling awe.
Hence all obedience bows to these alone,
And talent sinks, and merit weeps unknown;
Till time may come when stripped of all her charms,
The land of scholars and the nurse of arms,
Where noble stems transmit the patriot flame,

41

Where kings have toiled and poets wrote, for fame,
One sink of level avarice shall lie,
And scholars, soldiers, kings, unhonoured die.   360
    Yet think not, thus when Freedom's ills I state,
I mean to flatter kings, or court the great.
Ye powers of truth, that bid my soul aspire,
Far from my bosom drive the low desire!
And thou, fair Freedom, taught alike to feel
The rabble's rage and tyrant's angry steel:
Thou transitory flower, alike undone
By proud contempt or favour's fostering sun;
Still may thy blooms the changeful clime endure,
I only would repress them to secure;   370
For just experience tells, in every soil,
That those who think must govern those that toil;
And all that Freedom's highest aims can reach,
Is but to lay proportioned loads on each.
Hence, should one order disproportioned grow,
Its double weight must ruin all below.
    Oh, then how blind to all that truth requires,
Who think it freedom when a part aspires!
Calm is my soul, nor apt to rise in arms,
Except when fast-approaching danger warms: 380
But when contending chiefs blockade the throne,
Contracting regal power to stretch their own;
When I behold a factious band agree
To call it freedom when themselves are free;
Each wanton judge new penal statutes draw,
Laws grind the poor and rich men rule the law;
The wealth of climes, where savage nations roam,
Pillaged from slaves to purchase slaves at home;
Fear, pity, justice, indignation start,
Tear off reserve and bare my swelling heart;   390
Till half a patriot, half a coward grown,
I fly from petty tyrants to the throne.
    Yes, brother, curse with me that baleful hour,

When first ambition struck at regal power;
And thus polluting honour in its source,
Gave wealth to sway the mind with double force.
Have we not seen, round Britain's peopled shore,
Her useful sons exchanged for useless ore?
Seen all her triumphs but destruction haste,
Like flaring tapers brightening as they waste;   400
Seen Opulence, her grandeur to maintain,
Lead stern Depopulation in her train,
And over fields where scattered hamlets rose,
In barren solitary pomp repose?
Have we not seen at Pleasure's lordly call,
The smiling long-frequented village fall?
Beheld the duteous son, the sire decayed,
The modest matron and the blushing maid,
Forced from their homes, a melancholy train,
To traverse climes beyond the western main;   410
Where wild Oswego spreads her swamps around,
And Niagara stuns with thundering sound?
   Even now, perhaps, as there some pilgrim strays
Through tangled forests and through dangerous ways,
Where beasts with man divided empire claim,
And the brown Indian marks with murderous aim;
There, while above the giddy tempest flies,
And all around distressful yells arise,
The pensive exile, bending with his woe,
To stop too fearful, and too faint to go,   420
Casts a long look where England's glories shine,
And bids his bosom sympathise with mine.
   Vain, very vain, my weary search to find
That bliss which only centres in the mind:
Why have I strayed from pleasure and repose,
To seek a good each government bestows?
In every government, though terrors reign,
Though tyrant kings or tyrant laws restrain,
How small, of all that human hearts endure,

That part which laws or kings can cause or cure
Still to ourselves in every place consigned,
Our own felicity we make or find:
With secret course, which no loud storms annoy,
Glides the smooth current of domestic joy.
The lifted axe, the agonizing wheel,
Luke's iron crown and Damien's bed of steel,
To men remote from power but rarely known,
Leave reason, faith and conscience, all our own.

A New Simile
(in the manner of Swift)

Long had I sought in vain to find
A likeness for the scribbling kind;
The modern scribbling kind, who write
In wit and sense and nature's spite:
Till reading, I forget what day on,
A chapter out of Tooke's Pantheon,
I think I met with something there,
To suit my purpose to a hair.
But let us not proceed too furious:
First please to turn to god Mercurius:
You'll find him pictured at full length
In book the second, page the tenth:
The stress of all my proofs on him I lay,
And now proceed we to our simile.
    Imprimis, pray observe his hat,
Wings upon either side – mark that.
Well! what is it from thence we gather?
Why, these denote a brain of feather.
A brain of feather! very right,
With wit that's flighty, learning light;

Such as to modern bards decreed:
A just comparison, – proceed.

  In the next place, his feet peruse,
Wings grow again from both his shoes;
Designed, no doubt, their part to bear,
And waft his godship through the air;
And here my simile unites,
For in a modern poet's flights,
I'm sure it may be justly said,
His feet are useful as his head.

  Lastly, vouchsafe to observe his hand,
Filled with a snake-encircled wand;
By classic authors termed Caduceus,
And highly famed for several uses.
To wit, most wondrously endued,
No poppy-water half so good;
For let folks only get a touch,
Its soporific virtue's such,
Though ne'er so much awake before,
That quickly they begin to snore:
Add too, what certain writers tell,
With this he drives men's souls to hell.

  Now to apply, begin we then;
His wand's a modern author's pen;
The serpents round about it twined
Denote him of the reptile kind;
Denote the rage with which he writes,
His frothy slaver, venomed bites;
An equal semblance still to keep,
Alike too both conduce to sleep.
This difference only; as the god
Drove souls to Tartarus with his rod,
With his goose-quill the scribbling elf,
Instead of others, damns himself.

  And here my simile almost tripped;
Yet grant a word by way of postscript.

Moreover, Mercury had a failing:
Well! what of that? out with it – stealing;
In which all modern bards agree,
Being each as great a thief as he.
But even this deity's existence
Shall lend my simile assistance.
Our modern bards! why, what a pox
Are they but senseless stones and blocks?

Verses in Reply to an Invitation to Dinner at Dr Baker's

Your mandate I got,
You may all go to pot;
Had your senses been right,
You'd have sent before night;
As I hope to be saved,
I put off being shaved;
For I could not make bold,
While the matter was cold,
To meddle in suds,
Or to put on my duds;
So tell Horneck and Nesbitt,
And Baker and his bit,
And Kauffmann beside,
And the Jessamy bride,
With the rest of the crew,
The Reynoldses two,
Little Comedy's face,
And the Captain in lace,
(By the bye you may tell him,
I have something to sell him;
Of use I insist,
When he comes to enlist.

Your worships must know
That a few days ago,
An order went out,
For the footguards so stout
To wear tails in high taste,
Twelve inches at least:
Now I've got him a scale
To measure each tail,
To lengthen a short tail,
And a long one to curtail).
    Yet how can I when vexed,
Thus stray from my text?
Tell each other to rue
Your Devonshire crew,
For sending so late
To one of my state.
But 'tis Reynolds's way
From wisdom to stray,
And Angelica's whim
To be frolic like him,
But, alas! your good worships, how could they be wiser,
When both have been spoiled in today's *Advertiser*?

Epitaph on Edward Purdon

Here lies poor Ned Purdon, from misery freed,
   Who long was a bookseller's hack;
He led such a damnable life in this world, –
   I don't think he'll wish to come back.

Epilogue
to "The Good-natured Man"

As puffing quacks some caitiff wretch procure
To swear the pill or drop has wrought a cure;
Thus on the stage our play-wrights still depend
For Epilogues and Prologues on some friend,
Who knows each art of coaxing up the town,
And makes full many a bitter pill go down.
Conscious of this, our bard has gone about,
And teased each rhyming friend to help him out.
"An Epilogue – things can't go on without it;
It could not fail, would you but set about it."
"Young man," cries one – a bard laid up in clover –
"Alas, young man, my writing days are over;
Let boys play tricks, and kick the straw, not I;
Your brother Doctor there, perhaps may try." –
"What I? dear sir?" the Doctor interposes;
"What, plant my thistle, sir, among his roses!
No, no, I've other contests to maintain;
To-night I head our troops at Warwick Lane.
Go, ask your manager." – "Who, me? your pardon;
Those things are not our forte at Covent Garden."
Our author's friends, thus placed at happy distance,
Give him good words indeed, but no assistance.
As some unhappy wight, at some new play,
At the pit-door stands elbowing a way,
While oft, with many a smile, and many a shrug,
He eyes the centre, where his friends sit snug;
His simpering friends, with pleasure in their eyes,
Sink as he sinks, and as he rises rise:
He nods, they nod; he cringes, they grimace;
But not a soul will budge to give him place.
Since then, unhelped, our bard must now conform,
'To 'bide the pelting of this pitiless storm,'
Blame where you must, be candid where you can,
And be each critic the Good-Natured Man.

Epilogue
to the comedy of "The Sister"

What! five long acts – and all to make us wiser!
Our authoress sure has wanted an adviser.
Had she consulted *me*, she should have made
Her moral play a speaking masquerade;
Warmed up each bustling scene, and in her rage
Have emptied all the green-room on the stage.
My life on't, this had kept her play from sinking,
Have pleased our eyes and saved the pain of thinking.
Well, since she thus has shown her want of skill,
What if I give a masquerade? – I will.
But how? ay, there's the rub! [*pausing*] – I've got my cue;
The world's a masquerade; the masquers, you, you, you.
                              [*To Boxes, Pit, and Gallery.*
Lud! what a group the motley scene discloses!
False wits, false wives, false virgins, and false spouses!
Statesmen with bridles on; and, close beside 'em,
Patriots, in party-coloured suits, that ride 'em.
There Hebes turned of fifty try once more
To raise a flame in Cupids of threescore.
These in their turn, with appetites as keen,
Deserting fifty, fasten on fifteen.
Miss, not yet full fifteen, with fire uncommon,
Flings down her sampler, and takes up the woman:
The little urchin smiles, and spreads her lure,
And tries to kill ere she's got power to cure.
Thus 'tis with all – their chief and constant care
Is to seem everything but what they are.
Yon broad, bold, angry spark, I fix my eye on,
Who seems to have robbed his visor from the lion,
Who frowns, and talks, and swears, with round parade,
Looking, as who should say, *Dam'me! who's afraid?*
                              [*Mimicking.*
Strip but his visor off, and sure I am

49

You'll find his lionship a very lamb.
Yon politician, famous in debate,
Perhaps, to vulgar eyes, bestrides the state;
Yet, when he deigns his real shape to assume,
He turns old woman, and bestrides a broom.
Yon patriot, too, who presses on your sight,
And seems to every gazer all in white,
If with a bribe his candour you attack,
He bows, turns round, and whip – the man's a black!
Yon critic, too – but whither do I run?
If I proceed, our bard will be undone!
Well, then, a truce, since she requests it too;
Do you spare her, and I'll for once spare you.

The Deserted Village

Sweet Auburn, loveliest village of the plain,
Where health and plenty cheered the labouring swain,
Where smiling Spring its earliest visit paid,
And parting Summer's lingering blooms delayed:
Dear lovely bowers of innocence and ease,
Seats of my youth, when every sport could please:
How often have I loitered o'er thy green,
Where humble happiness endeared each scene;
How often have I paused on every charm,
The sheltered cot, the cultivated farm,   10
The never-failing brook, the busy mill,
The decent church that topped the neighbouring hill;
The hawthorn bush, with seats beneath the shade,
For talking age and whispering lovers made.
How often have I blessed the coming day,
When toil remitting lent its turn to play,
And all the village train, from labour free,
Led up their sports beneath the spreading tree.
While many a pastime circled in the shade,
The young contending as the old surveyed;   20
And many a gambol frolicked o'er the ground,
And sleights of art and feats of strength went round;
And still, as each repeated pleasure tired,
Succeeding sports the mirthful band inspired;
The dancing pair that simply sought renown,
By holding out to tire each other down;
The swain mistrustless of his smutted face,
While secret laughter tittered round the place;
The bashful virgin's side-long looks of love;
The matron's glance, that would those looks reprove: 30
These were thy charms, sweet village; sports like these,
With sweet succession, taught even toil to please;
These round thy bowers their cheerful influence shed,
These were thy charms – but all these charms are fled.

Sweet smiling village, loveliest of the lawn,
Thy sports are fled, and all thy charms withdrawn;
Amidst thy bowers the tyrant's hand is seen,
And desolation saddens all thy green:
One only master grasps the whole domain,
And half a village stints thy smiling plain: 40
No more thy glassy brook reflects the day,
But, choked with sedges, works its weedy way:
Along thy grades, a solitary guest,
The hollow-sounding bittern guards its nest;
Amidst thy desert walks the lapwing flies,
And tires their echoes with unvaried cries:
Sunk are thy bowers in shapeless ruin all,
And the long grass o'ertops the mouldering wall;
And, trembling, shrinking from the spoiler's hand,
Far, far away, thy children leave the land.   50
    Ill fares the land, to hastening ills a prey,
Where wealth accumulates, and men decay.
Princes and lords may flourish, or may fade;
A breath can make them, as a breath has made;
But a bold peasantry, their country's pride,
When once destroyed, can never be supplied.
    A time there was, ere England's griefs began,
When every rood of ground maintained its man;
For him light labour spread her wholesome store,
Just gave what life required, but gave no more: 60
His best companions, innocence and health;
And his best riches, ignorance of wealth.
    But times are altered; trade's unfeeling train
Usurp the land, and dispossess the swain;
Along the lawn, where scattered hamlets rose,
Unwieldy wealth and cumbrous pomp repose;
And every want to luxury allied,
And every pang that folly pays to pride.
Those gentle hours that plenty bade to bloom,
Those calm desires that asked but little room,   70

Those healthful sports that graced the peaceful scene,
Lived in each look and brightened all the green;
These, far departing, seek a kinder shore,
And rural mirth and manners are no more.
   Sweet Auburn! parent of the blissful hour,
Thy glades forlorn confess the tyrant's power.
Here, as I take my solitary rounds,
Amidst thy tangling walks and ruined grounds,
And, many a year elapsed, return to view
Where once the cottage stood, the hawthorn grew,   80
Remembrance wakes with all her busy train,
Swells at my breast and turns the past to pain.
   In all my wanderings through this world of care,
In all my griefs – and God has given my share –
I still had hopes, my latest hours to crown,
Amidst these humble bowers to lay me down;
To husband out life's taper at the close,
And keep the flame from wasting by repose:
I still had hopes, for pride attends us still,
Amidst the swains to show my book-learned skill,   90
Around my fire an evening group to draw,
And tell of all I felt and all I saw;
And, as a hare, whom hounds and horns pursue,
Pants to the place from whence at first she flew,
I still had hopes, my long vexations past,
Here to return – and die at home at last.
   O blest retirement, friend to life's decline,
Retreat from care, that never must be mine,
How blest is he who crowns, in shades like these,
A youth of labour with an age of ease;   100
Who quits a world where strong temptations try,
And, since 'tis hard to combat, learns to fly:
For him no wretches, born to work and weep,
Explore the mine, or tempt the dangerous deep;
No surly porter stands in guilty state
To spurn imploring famine from the gate;

But on he moves to meet his latter end,
Angels around befriending virtue's friend;
Sinks to the grave with unperceived decay,
While resignation gently slopes the way;   110
And, all his prospects brightening to the last,
His heaven commences ere the world be past!
   Sweet was the sound, when oft at evening's close
Up yonder hill the village murmur rose;
There, as I passed with careless steps and slow,
The mingled notes came softened from below;
The swain responsive as the milk-maid sung,
The sober herd that lowed to meet their young;
The noisy geese that gabbled o'er the pool,
The playful children just let loose from school;   120
The watch-dog's voice that bayed the whispering wind,
And the loud laugh that spoke the vacant mind:
These all in sweet confusion sought the shade,
And filled each pause the nightingale had made.
But now the sounds of population fail,
No cheerful murmurs fluctuate in the gale,
No busy steps the grass-grown footway tread,
But all the blooming flush of life is fled:
All but yon widowed solitary thing,
That feebly bends beside the plashy spring;   130
She, wretched matron, forced, in age, for bread,
To strip the brook with mantling cresses spread,
To pick her wintry faggot from the thorn,
To seek her nightly shed and weep till morn;
She only left of all the harmless train,
The sad historian of the pensive plain.
   Near yonder copse, where once the garden smiled,
And still where many a garden-flower grows wild,
There, where a few torn shrubs the place disclose,
The village preacher's modest mansion rose.   140
A man he was to all the country dear,
And passing rich with forty pounds a year;

54

Remote from towns he ran his godly race,
Nor e'er had changed, nor wished to change, his place;
Unskilful he to fawn, or seek for power
By doctrines fashioned to the varying hour;
Far other aims his heart had learned to prize,
More skilled to raise the wretched than to rise.
His house was known to all the vagrant train,
He chid their wanderings, but relieved their pain;
The long-remembered beggar was his guest,
Whose beard descending swept his aged breast;
The ruined spendthrift, now no longer proud,
Claimed kindred there, and had his claims allowed;
The broken soldier, kindly bade to stay,
Sat by his fire and talked the night away;
Wept o'er his wounds or tales of sorrow done,
Shouldered his crutch and showed how fields were won.
Pleased with his guests, the good man learned to glow,
And quite forgot their vices in their woe;
Careless their merits or their faults to scan,
His pity gave ere charity began.
    Thus to relieve the wretched was his pride,
And even his failings leaned to virtue's side;
But in his duty prompt at every call,
He watched and wept, he prayed and felt, for all:
And, as a bird each fond endearment tries
To tempt its new-fledged offspring to the skies,
He tried each art, reproved each dull delay,
Allured to brighter worlds and led the way.
    Beside the bed where parting life was laid,
And sorrow, guilt, and pain by turns dismayed,
The reverend champion stood. At his control,
Despair and anguish fled the struggling soul;
Comfort came down the trembling wretch to raise,
And his last faltering accents whispered praise.
    At church, with meek and unaffected grace,
His looks adorned the venerable place;

55

Truth from his lips prevailed with double sway,
And fools, who came to scoff, remained to pray.   180
The service past, around the pious man,
With steady zeal, each honest rustic ran;
Even children followed with endearing wile,
And plucked his gown, to share the good man's smile;
His ready smile a parent's warmth expressed;
Their welfare pleased him, and their cares distressed;
To them his heart, his love, his griefs were given,
But all his serious thoughts had rest in Heaven.
As some tall cliff, that lifts its awful form,
Swells from the vale and midway leaves the storm,   190
Though round its breast the rolling clouds are spread,
Eternal sunshine settles on its head.
    Beside yon straggling fence that skirts the way,
With blossomed furze unprofitably gay,
There, in his noisy mansion, skilled to rule,
The village master taught his little school;
A man severe he was, and stern to view:
I knew him well, and every truant knew;
Well had the boding tremblers learned to trace
The day's disasters in his morning face;   200
Full well they laughed with counterfeited glee
At all his jokes, for many a joke had he;
Full well the busy whisper, circling round,
Conveyed the dismal tidings when he frowned;
Yet he was kind, or if severe in aught,
The love he bore to learning was in fault;
The village all declared how much he knew;
'Twas certain he could write, and cipher too;
Lands he could measure, terms and tides presage,
And even the story ran that he could gauge.   210
In arguing, too, the parson owned his skill,
For even though vanquished, he could argue still;
While words of learned length and thundering sound
Amazed the gazing rustics ranged around;

56

And still they gazed, and still the wonder grew,
That one small head should carry all he knew.
   But past is all his fame. The very spot,
Where many a time he triumphed, is forgot.
Near yonder thorn, that lifts its head on high,
Where once the sign-post caught the passing eye,   220
Low lies that house where nut-brown draughts inspired,
Where gray-beard mirth and smiling toil retired;
Where village statesmen talked with looks profound,
And news much older than their ale went round.
Imagination fondly stoops to trace
The parlour splendours of that festive place;
The whitewashed wall, the nicely-sanded floor,
The varnished clock that clicked behind the door;
The chest, contrived a double debt to pay,
A bed by night, a chest of drawers by day;   230
The pictures placed for ornament and use,
The twelve good rules, the royal game of goose;
The hearth, except when winter chilled the day,
With aspen boughs, and flowers, and fennel, gay;
While broken tea-cups, wisely kept for show,
Ranged o'er the chimney, glistened in a row.
   Vain transitory splendours! could not all
Reprieve the tottering mansion from its fall?
Obscure it sinks, nor shall it more impart
An hour's impatience to the poor man's heart.   240
Thither no more the peasant shall repair
To sweet oblivion of his daily care;
No more the farmer's news, the barber's tale,
No more the woodman's ballad shall prevail;
No more the smith his dusky brow shall clear,
Relax his ponderous strength and lean to hear;
The host himself no longer shall be found
Careful to see the mantling bliss go round;
Nor the coy maid, half willing to be prest,
Shall kiss the cup to pass it to the rest.   250

57

Yes! let the rich deride, the proud disdain,
These simple blessings of the lowly train;
To me more dear, congenial to my heart,
One native charm than all the gloss of art.
Spontaneous joys, where nature has its play,
The soul adopts and owns their first-born sway;
Lightly they frolic o'er the vacant mind,
Unenvied, unmolested, unconfined:
But the long pomp, the midnight masquerade,
With all the freaks of wanton wealth arrayed,   260
In these, ere triflers half their wish obtain,
The toiling pleasure sickens into pain;
And, even while Fashion's brightest arts decoy
The heart distrusting asks, if this be joy.
    Ye friends to truth, ye statesmen, who survey
The rich man's joys increase, the poor's decay,
'Tis yours to judge how wide the limits stand
Between a splendid and a happy land.
Proud swells the tide with loads of freighted ore,
And shouting Folly hails them from her shore;   270
Hoards, even beyond the miser's wish, abound,
And rich men flock from all the world around.
Yet count our gains. This wealth is but a name
That leaves our useful products still the same.
Not so the loss. The man of wealth and pride
Takes up a space that many poor supplied;
Space for his lake, his park's extended bounds,
Space for his horses, equipage, and hounds;
The robe that wraps his limbs in silken sloth,
Has robbed the neighbouring fields of half their growth;   280
His seat, where solitary sports are seen,
Indignant spurns the cottage from the green;
Around the world each needful product flies,
For all the luxuries the world supplies;
While thus the land, adorned for pleasure all,
In barren splendour feebly waits the fall.

As some fair female, unadorned and plain,
Secure to please while youth confirms her reign,
Slights every borrowed charm that dress supplies,
Nor shares with art the triumph of her eyes;   290
But when those charms are past, for charms are frail,
When time advances and when lovers fail,
She then shines forth, solicitous to bless,
In all the glaring impotence of dress:
Thus fares the land, by luxury betrayed,
In nature's simplest charms at first arrayed;
But verging to decline, its splendours rise,
Its vistas strike, its palaces surprise;
While scourged by famine from the smiling land
The mournful peasant leads his humble band;   300
And while he sinks, without one arm to save,
The country blooms – a garden and a grave.
    Where, then, ah! where, shall poverty reside,
To 'scape the pressure of contiguous pride?
If to some common's fenceless limits strayed,
He drives his flock to pick the scanty blade,
Those fenceless fields the sons of wealth divide,
And even the bare-worn common is denied.
    If to the city sped – what waits him there?
To see profusion that he must not share;   310
To see ten thousand baneful arts combined
To pamper luxury and thin mankind;
To see each joy the sons of pleasure know
Extorted from his fellow-creature's woe:
Here, while the courtier glitters in brocade,
There the pale artist plies the sickly trade;
Here while the proud their long-drawn pomps display,
There the black gibbet glooms beside the way:
The dome where Pleasure holds her midnight reign,
Here, richly decked, admits the gorgeous train;   320
Tumultuous grandeur crowds the blazing square,
The rattling chariots clash, the torches glare.

Sure scenes like these no troubles e'er annoy!
Sure these denote one universal joy! –
Are these thy serious thoughts? – ah, turn thine eyes
Where the poor houseless shivering female lies:
She, once, perhaps, in village plenty blessed,
Has wept at tales of innocence distressed;
Her modest looks the cottage might adorn,
Sweet as the primrose peeps beneath the thorn: 330
Now lost to all, her friends, her virtue, fled,
Near her betrayer's door she lays her head,
And pinched with cold and shrinking from the shower,
With heavy heart deplores that luckless hour,
When idly first, ambitious of the town,
She left her wheel and robes of country brown.
    Do thine, sweet Auburn, thine, the loveliest train,
Do thy fair tribes participate her pain?
Even now, perhaps, by cold and hunger led,
At proud men's doors they ask a little bread!   340
    Ah, no. To distant climes, a dreary scene,
Where half the convex world intrudes between,
Through torrid tracts with fainting steps they go,
Where wild Altama murmurs to their woe.
Far different there from all that charmed before
The various terrors of that horrid shore;
Those blazing suns that dart a downward ray,
And fiercely shed intolerable day;
Those matted woods where birds forget to sing,
But silent bats in drowsy clusters cling;   350
Those poisonous fields with rank luxuriance crowned,
Where the dark scorpion gathers death around;
Where at each step the stranger fears to wake
The rattling terrors of the vengeful snake;
Where crouching tigers wait their hapless prey,
And savage men more murderous still than they;
While oft in whirls the mad tornado flies,
Mingling the ravaged landscape with the skies.

Far different these from every former scene,
The cooling brook, the grassy-vested green,   360
The breezy covert of the warbling grove,
That only sheltered thefts of harmless love.
   Good Heaven! what sorrows gloomed that parting day,
That called them from their native walks away;
When the poor exiles, every pleasure past,
Hung round the bowers and fondly looked their last,
And took a long farewell and wished in vain
For seats like these beyond the western main;
And shuddering still to face the distant deep,
Returned and wept, and still returned to weep.   370
The good old sire the first prepared to go
To new-found worlds, and wept for others' woe;
But for himself, in conscious virtue brave,
He only wished for worlds beyond the grave.
His lovely daughter, lovelier in her tears,
The fond companion of his helpless years,
Silent went next, neglectful of her charms,
And left a lover's for a father's arms.
With louder plaints the mother spoke her woes,
And blessed the cot where every pleasure rose,   380
And kissed her thoughtless babes with many a tear,
And clasped them close, in sorrow doubly dear;
Whilst her fond husband strove to lend relief
In all the silent manliness of grief.
   O Luxury! thou cursed by Heaven's decree,
How ill exchanged are things like these for thee!
How do thy potions, with insidious joy,
Diffuse their pleasures only to destroy!
Kingdoms by thee to sickly greatness grown,
Boast of a florid vigour not their own;   390
At every draught more large and large they grow,
A bloated mass of rank unwieldy woe;
Till sapped their strength and every part unsound,
Down, down they sink, and spread a ruin round.

61

Even now the devastation is begun,
And half the business of destruction done;
Even now, methinks, as pondering here I stand,
I see the rural Virtues leave the land.
Down where yon anchoring vessel spreads the sail,
That idly waiting flaps with every gale,   400
Downward they move, a melancholy band,
Pass from the shore and darken all the strand.
Contented Toil, and hospitable Care,
And kind connubial Tenderness are there;
And Piety with wishes placed above,
And steady Loyalty, and faithful Love.
    And thou, sweet Poetry, thou loveliest maid,
Still first to fly where sensual joys invade:
Unfit, in these degenerate times of shame,
To catch the heart or strike for honest fame;   410
Dear charming nymph, neglected and decried,
My shame in crowds, my solitary pride;
Thou source of all my bliss and all my woe,
That found'st me poor at first and keep'st me so;
Thou guide by which the nobler arts excel,
Thou nurse of every virtue, fare thee well!
Farewell, and oh, where'er thy voice be tried,
On Torno's cliffs or Pambamarca's side,
Whether where equinoctial fervours glow,
Or winter wraps the polar world in snow,   420
Still let thy voice, prevailing over time,
Redress the rigours of the inclement clime;
Aid slighted Truth; with thy persuasive strain
Teach erring man to spurn the rage of gain;
Teach him that states, of native strength possessed,
Though very poor, may still be very blest;
That Trade's proud empire hastes to swift decay,
As ocean sweeps the laboured mole away;
While self-dependent power can time defy,
As rocks resist the billows and the sky.   430

Epitaph on Dr Parnell

This tomb, inscribed to gentle Parnell's name,
May speak our gratitude, but not his fame.
What heart but feels his sweetly-moral lay,
That leads to truth through pleasure's flowery way!
Celestial themes confessed his tuneful aid;
And Heaven, that lent him genius, was repaid.
Needless to him the tribute we bestow,
The transitory breath of fame below:
More lasting rapture from his works shall rise,
While converts thank their poet in the skies.

The Haunch of Venison
a poetical epistle to Lord Clare

Thanks, my lord, for your venison, for finer or fatter
Never ranged in a forest or smoked on a platter;
The haunch was a picture for painters to study,
The fat was so white, and the lean was so ruddy.
Though my stomach was sharp, I could scarce help regretting
To spoil such a delicate picture by eating:
I had thoughts in my chamber to place it in view,
To be shown to my friends as a piece of *virtû*;
As in some Irish houses, where things are so-so,
One gammon of bacon hangs up for a show;   10
But, for eating a rasher of what they take pride in,
They'd as soon think of eating the pan it is fried in.
But hold – let us pause – don't I hear you pronounce,
This tale of the bacon's a damnable bounce?
Well, suppose it a bounce – sure a poet may try,
By a bounce now and then, to get courage to fly.
  But, my lord, it's no bounce: I protest in my turn,

It's a truth – and your lordship may ask Mr Burn.
To go on with my tale – as I gazed on the haunch,
I thought of a friend that was trusty and staunch,   20
So I cut it, and sent it to Reynolds undrest,
To paint it or eat it, just as he liked best.
Of the neck and the breast I had next to dispose,
'Twas a neck and a breast that might rival Monroe's:
But in parting with these I was puzzled again,
With the how, and the who, and the where, and the when.
There's Howard, and Coley, and Hogarth, and Hiff,
I think they love venison – I know they love beef.
There's my countryman Higgins – oh! let him alone,
For making a blunder, or picking a bone.   30
But hang it – to poets who seldom can eat,
Your very good mutton's a very good treat;
Such dainties to them their health it might hurt,
It's like sending them ruffles when wanting a shirt.
   While thus I debated, in reverie centred,
An acquaintance, a friend, as he called himself, entered;
An under-bred, fine-spoken fellow was he,
And he smiled as he looked at the venison and me.
"What have we got here? – why, this is good eating!
Your own, I suppose – or is it in waiting?"   40
"Why, whose should it be?" cried I, with a flounce:
"I get these things often" – but that was a bounce:
"Some lords, my acquaintance, that settle the nation,
Are pleased to be kind – but I hate ostentation."
   "If that be the case, then," cried he, very gay,
"I'm glad I have taken this house in my way.
To-morrow you take a poor dinner with me;
No words – I insist on't – precisely at three;
We'll have Johnson and Burke, all the wits will be there;
My acquaintance is slight or I'd ask my Lord Clare.   50
And now that I think on't, as I am a sinner,
We wanted this venison to make out the dinner.
What say you – a pasty? it shall, and it must,

64

And my wife, little Kitty, is famous for crust.
Here, porter! – this venison with me to Mile-End;
No stirring – I beg – my dear friend – my dear friend!"
Thus snatching his hat, he brushed off like the wind,
And the porter and eatables followed behind.
   Left alone to reflect, having emptied my shelf,
And "nobody with me at sea but myself;"   60
Though I could not help thinking my gentleman hasty,
Yet Johnson and Burke and a good venison pasty
Were things that I never disliked in my life,
Though clogged with a coxcomb and Kitty his wife.
So next day, in due splendour to make my approach,
I drove to his door in my own hackney coach.
   When come to the place where we all were to dine
(A chair-lumbered closet, just twelve feet by nine),
My friend bade me welcome, but struck me quite dumb
With tidings that Johnson and Burke could not come;   70
"For I knew it," he cried, "both eternally fail,
The one with his speeches, and t'other with Thrale;
But no matter, I'll warrant we'll make up the party,
With two full as clever and ten times as hearty;
The one is a Scotchman, the other a Jew,
They're both of them merry, and authors like you;
The one writes the *Snarler*, the other the *Scourge*;
Some think he writes *Cinna* – he owns to *Panurge*."
While thus he described them by trade and by name,
They enter'd, and dinner was served as they came.   80
   At the top a fried liver and bacon were seen;
At the bottom was tripe, in a swinging tureen;
At the sides there were spinach and pudding made hot;
In the middle a place where the pasty – was not.
Now, my lord, as for tripe, it's my utter aversion,
And your bacon I hate like a Turk or a Persian;
So there I sat stuck, like a horse in a pound,
While the bacon and liver went merrily round:
But what vexed me most, was that damned Scottish rogue,

With his long-winded speeches, his smiles and his brogue;   90
And, "Madam," quoth he, "may this bit be my poison,
A prettier dinner I never set eyes on;
Pray a slice of your liver though, may I be curst,
But I've ate of your tripe till I'm ready to burst."
"The tripe," quoth the Jew, with his chocolate cheek,
"I could dine on this tripe seven days in the week:
I like these here dinners so pretty and small;
But your friend there, the Doctor, eats nothing at all."
"O ho" quoth my friend, "he'll come on in a trice,
He's keeping a corner for something that's nice: 100
There's a pasty." – "A pasty!" repeated the Jew;
"I don't care if I keep a corner for't too."
"What the de'il, mon, a pasty!" re-echoed the Scot;
"Though splitting, I'll still keep a corner for thot."
"We'll all keep a corner," the lady cried out;
"We'll all keep a corner," was echoed about.
While thus we resolved, and the pasty delayed,
With looks that quite petrified, entered the maid;
A visage so sad, and so pale with affright,
Waked Priam in drawing his curtains by night.   110
But we quickly found out – for who could mistake her? –
That she came with some terrible news from the baker:
And so it fell out, for that negligent sloven
Had shut out the pasty on shutting his oven.
Sad Philomel thus – but let similes drop –
And now that I think on't, the story may stop.
   To be plain, my good lord, it's but labour misplaced,
To send such good verses to one of your taste:
You've got an odd something – a kind of discerning –
A relish – a taste – sickened over by learning;   120
At least, it's your temper, as very well known,
That you think very slightly of all that's your own:
So, perhaps, in your habits of thinking amiss,
You may make a mistake, and think slightly of this.

Prologue to "Zobeide"
a Tragedy written by Joseph Craddock

In these bold times, when Learning's sons explore
The distant climate and the savage shore;
When wise astronomers to India steer,
And quit for Venus many a brighter here;
While botanists, all cold to smiles and dimpling,
Forsake the fair and patiently – go simpling;
When every bosom swells with wondrous scenes,
Priests, cannibals, and hoity-toity queens:
Our bard into the general spirit enters,
And fits his little frigate for adventures:
With Scythian stores and trinkets deeply laden,
He this way steers his course, in hopes of trading:
Yet ere he lands has ordered me before,
To make an observation on the shore.
Where are we driven? our reckoning sure is lost!
This seems a rocky and a dangerous coast.
Lord, what a sultry climate am I under!
Yon ill-foreboding cloud seems big with thunder:

                                      [Upper Gallery.

There mangroves spread, and larger than I've seen 'em –

                                              [Pit.

Here trees of stately size, and turtles in 'em –

                                     [Balconies.

Here ill-conditioned oranges abound –   *[Stage.*
And apples, *bitter* apples, strew the ground:

                                      [Tasting them.

The inhabitants are cannibals, I fear:
I heard a hissing – there are serpents here!
Oh, there the natives are, a dreadful race!
The men have tails, the women paint the face!
No doubt they're all barbarians! – Yes, 'tis so.
I'll try to make palaver with them though.

                                      [making signs.

'Tis best, however, keeping at a distance.
Good savages, our captain craves assistance.
Our ship's well stored – in yonder creek we've laid her,
His honour is no mercenary trader.
This is his first adventure; lend him aid,
Or you may chance to spoil a thriving trade.
His goods, he hopes, are prime, and brought from far,
Equally fit for gallantry and war.
What, no reply to promises so ample?
– I'd best step back, and order up a sample.

Song
intended to have been sung in the comedy of "She Stoops to Conquer"

Ah me! when shall I marry me?
Lovers are plenty but fail to relieve me;
He, fond youth, that could carry me,
Offers to love but means to deceive me.

But I will rally and combat the ruiner:
Not a look, not a smile, shall my passion discover.
She that gives all to the false one pursuing her,
Makes but a penitent, loses a lover.

Epilogue
to "She Stoops to Conquer"

Well, having stooped to conquer with success,
And gained a husband without aid from dress,
Still as a barmaid, I could wish it too,
As I have conquered him, to conquer you:
And let me say, for all your resolution,

68

That pretty barmaids have done execution.
Our life is all a play, composed to please,
"We have our exits and our entrances."
The First Act shows the simple country maid,
Harmless and young, of everything afraid;
Blushes when hired, and with unmeaning action,
I hopes as how to give you satisfaction.
Her Second Act displays a livelier scene, –
The unblushing barmaid of a country inn,
Who whisks about the house, at market caters,
Talks loud, coquets the guests, and scolds the waiters.
Next the scene shifts to town, and there she soars,
The chop-house toast of ogling connoisseurs.
On squires and cits she there displays her arts,
And on the gridiron broils her lovers' hearts –
And as she smiles, her triumphs to complete,
Even common-councilmen forget to eat.
The Fourth Act shows her wedded to the squire,
And madam now begins to hold it higher;
Pretends to taste, at operas cries *Caro*,
And quits her *Nancy Dawson* for *Che Faro*;
Doats upon dancing and in all her pride
Swims round the room, the *Heinel* of Cheapside;
Ogles and leers with artificial skill,
Till, having lost in age the power to kill,
She sits all night at cards, and ogles at spadille.
Such, through our lives, the eventful history –
The Fifth and Last Act still remains for me.
The barmaid now for your protection prays,
Turns female barrister and pleads for Bayes.

Epilogue

spoken by Mr Lee Lewes, in the character of Harlequin, at his benefit

Hold! Prompter, hold! a word before your nonsense;
I'd speak a word or two, to ease my conscience.
My pride forbids it ever should be said
My heels eclipsed the honours of my head;
That I found humour in a piebald vest,
Or ever thought that jumping was a jest.

[*Takes off his mask.*

Whence and what art thou, visionary birth?
Nature disowns and Reason scorns thy mirth;
In thy black aspect every passion sleeps,
The joy that dimples and the woe that weeps.
How hast thou filled the scene with all thy brood,
Of fools pursuing, and of fools pursued!
Whose ins and outs no ray of sense discloses;
Whose only plot it is to break our noses;
Whilst from below the trap-door demons rise,
And from above the dangling deities.
And shall I mix in this unhallowed crew?
May rosined lightning blast me, if I do!
No – I will act, I'll vindicate the stage:
Shakespeare himself shall feel my tragic rage.
"Off! off! vile trappings!" a new passion reigns!
The maddening monarch revels in my veins.
Oh for a Richard's voice to catch the theme:
"Give me another horse! bind up my wounds! – soft – 'twas but
      a dream."
Ay, 'twas but a dream, for now there's no retreating:
If I cease Harlequin, I cease from eating.
'Twas thus that Æsop's stag, a creature blameless,
Yet something vain, like one that shall be nameless,
Once on the margin of a fountain stood,
And cavilled at his image in the flood.
"The deuce confound," he cries, "these drumstick shanks!

70

They neither have my gratitude nor thanks;
They're perfectly disgraceful, strike me dead!
But for a head – yes, yes, I have a head.
How piercing is that eye! how sleek that brow!
My horns! I'm told horns are the fashion now."
Whilst thus he spoke, astonished, to his view,
Near and more near the hounds and huntsmen drew.
"Hoicks! hark forward!" came thundering from behind;
He bounds aloft, outstrips the fleeting wind:
He quits the woods, and tries the beaten ways;
He starts, he pants, he takes the circling maze.
At length his silly head, so prized before,
Is taught his former folly to deplore;
Whilst his strong limbs conspire to set him free,
And at one bound he saves himself, like me,

     [Taking a jump through the stage-door.

Retaliation
a poem

Of old, when Scarron his companions invited,
Each guest brought his dish and the feast was united.
If our landlord[1] supplies us with beef and with fish,
Let each guest bring himself, and he brings the best dish.
Our Dean[2] shall be venison, just fresh from the plains;
Our Burke[3] shall be tongue, with a garnish of brains;
Our Will[4] shall be wild-fowl, of excellent flavour;
And Dick[5] with his pepper shall heighten their savour;

---

[1] the master of St James's Coffee-house, where the doctor and the friends he has characterised in this poem, occasionally dined. [2] Dr Barnard, Dean of Derry, in Ireland [3] Mr Edmund Burke. [4] Mr William Burke, late secretary to General Conway, and member for Bedwin. [5] Mr Richard Burke, Collector of Granada.

Our Cumberland's[6] sweetbread its place shall obtain,
And Douglas[7] is pudding, substantial and plain: 10
Our Garrick's[8] a salad; for in him we see
Oil, vinegar, sugar, and saltness agree:
To make out the dinner, full certain I am,
That Ridge[9] is anchovy, and Reynolds[10] is lamb;
That Hickey's[11] a capon; and by the same rule,
Magnanimous Goldsmith a gooseberry fool.
At a dinner so various, at such a repast,
Who'd not be a glutton and stick to the last?
Here, waiter, more wine, let me sit while I'm able,
Till all my companions sink under the table;   20
Then, with chaos and blunders encircling my head,
Let me ponder and tell what I think of the dead.
    Here lies the good Dean, re-united to earth,
Who mixed reason with pleasure and wisdom with mirth;
If he had any faults, he has left us in doubt;
At least, in six weeks I could not find 'em out;
Yet some have declared, and it can't be denied 'em,
That sly-boots was cursedly cunning to hide 'em.
    Here lies our good Edmund, whose genius was such,
We scarcely can praise it or blame it too much;   30
Who, born for the universe, narrowed his mind,
And to party gave up what was meant for mankind;
Though fraught with all learning, yet straining his throat
To persuade Tommy Townshend[12] to lend him a vote;
Who, too deep for his hearers, still went on refining,
And thought of convincing, while they thought of dining:

[6] Mr Richard Cumberland, author of *The West Indian*, *The Fashionable Lover*, *The Brothers*, and other dramatic pieces.   [7] Canon of Windsor, an ingenious Scotch gentleman, who has no less distinguished himself as a citizen of the world, than a sound critic, in detecting several literary mistakes (or rather forgeries) of his countrymen; particularly Lauder on Milton, and Bower's History of the Popes. [8] David Garrick.   [9] Counsellor John Ridge, a gentleman belonging to the Irish bar. [10] Sir Joshua Reynolds.   [11] an eminent attorney.   [12] Mr T. Townshend, member for Whitchurch.

Though equal to all things, for all things unfit;
Too nice for a statesman, too proud for a wit;
For a patriot too cool; for a drudge disobedient;
And too fond of the *right* to pursue the *expedient*.   40
In short, 'twas his fate, unemployed or in place, sir,
To eat mutton cold, and cut blocks with a razor.
　　Here lies honest William, whose heart was a mint,
While the owner ne'er knew half the good that was in't:
The pupil of impulse, it forced him along,
His conduct still right, with his argument wrong;
Still aiming at honour, yet fearing to roam,
The coachman was tipsy, the chariot drove home.
Would you ask for his merits? – alas! he had none;
What was good was spontaneous, his faults were his own.   50
　　Here lies honest Richard,[13] whose fate I must sigh at;
Alas! that such frolic should now be so quiet!
What spirits were his, what wit and what whim!
Now breaking a jest and now breaking a limb!
Now wrangling and grumbling to keep up the ball,
Now teasing and vexing, yet laughing at all.
In short, so provoking a devil was Dick,
We wished him full ten times a day at Old Nick;
But, missing his mirth and agreeable vein,
As often we wished to have Dick back again.   60
　　Here Cumberland lies, having acted his parts,
The Terence of England, the mender of hearts;
A flattering painter, who made it his care
To draw men as they ought to be, not as they are.
His gallants are all faultless, his women divine,
And Comedy wonders at being so fine:
Like a tragedy queen he has dizened her out,
Or rather like Tragedy giving a rout.

---

[13] Mr Richard Burke. This gentleman having slightly fractured one of his arms
and one of his legs, at different times, the doctor has rallied him on those acci-
dents, as a kind of retributive justice for breaking his jests upon other people.

His fools have their follies so lost in a crowd
Of virtues and feelings, that Folly grows proud; 70
And coxcombs, alike in their failings alone,
Adopting his portraits, are pleased with their own.
Say, where has our poet this malady caught?
Or wherefore his characters thus without fault?
Say, was it that vainly directing his view
To find out men's virtues, and finding them few,
Quite sick of pursuing each troublesome elf,
He grew lazy at last, and drew from himself?
  Here Douglas retires from his toils to relax,
The scourge of impostors, the terror of quacks; 80
Come, all ye quack bards, and ye quacking divines,
Come, and dance on the spot where your tyrant reclines.
When satire and censure encircled his throne,
I feared for your safety, I fear'd for my own:
But now he is gone, and we want a detector,
Our Dodds[14] shall be pious, our Kenricks[15] shall lecture;
Macpherson[16] write bombast, and call it a style;
Our Townshend make speeches, and I shall compile;
New Lauders and Bowers the Tweed shall cross over,
No countryman living their tricks to discover; 90
Detection her taper shall quench to a spark,
And Scotchman meet Scotchman and cheat in the dark.
  Here lies David Garrick, describe him who can,
An abridgment of all that was pleasant in man;
As an actor, confessed without rival to shine;
As a wit, if not first, in the very first line:
Yet, with talents like these and an excellent heart,
The man had his failings – a dupe to his art.
Like an ill-judging beauty, his colours he spread,
And beplastered with rouge his own natural red. 100

[14] the Rev. Dr Dodd.   [15] Dr Kenrick, who read lectures at the Devil Tavern, under the title of 'The School of Shakespeare'.   [16] James Macpherson, Esq., lately, from the mere force of his style, wrote down the first poet of all antiquity.

On the stage he was natural, simple, affecting;
'Twas only that when he was off he was acting.
With no reason on earth to go out of his way,
He turn'd and he varied full ten times a day;
Though secure of our hearts, yet confoundedly sick,
If they were not his own by finessing and trick:
He cast off his friends, as a huntsman his pack,
For he knew when he pleased he could whistle them back.
Of praise a mere glutton, he swallowed what came,
And the puff of a dunce, he mistook it for fame; 110
Till his relish grown callous, almost to disease,
Who peppered the highest was surest to please.
But let us be candid, and speak out our mind:
If dunces applauded, he paid them in kind.
Ye Kenricks, ye Kellys[17] and Woodfalls[18] so grave,
What a commerce was yours, while you got and you gave!
How did Grub Street re-echo the shouts that you raised,
While he was be-Rosciused and you were be-praised!
But peace to his spirit, wherever it flies,
To act as an angel and mix with the skies: 120
Those poets who owe their best fame to his skill
Shall still be his flatterers, go where he will.
Old Shakespeare, receive him with praise and with love,
And Beaumonts and Bens be his Kellys above.

   Here Hickey reclines, a most blunt, pleasant creature,
And slander itself must allow him good-nature:
He cherished his friend, and he relished a bumper;
Yet one fault he had, and that one a thumper.
Perhaps you may ask if the man was a miser?
I answer, no, no, for he always was wiser: 130
Too courteous, perhaps, or obligingly flat?
His very worst foe can't accuse him of that.
Perhaps he confided in men as they go,

---

[17] Mr Hugh Kelly, author of *False Delicacy, Word to the Wise, Clementina, School for Wives*, &c. [18] Mr W. Woodfall, printer of the *Morning Chronicle*.

And so was too foolishly honest? Ah, no!
Then what was his failing? come, tell it, and burn ye, –
He was – could he help it? – a special attorney.
   Here Reynolds is laid, and, to tell you my mind,
He has not left a better or wiser behind:
His pencil was striking, resistless and grand;
His manners were gentle, complying and bland;   140
Still born to improve us in every part,
His pencil our faces, his manners our heart;
To coxcombs averse, yet most civilly steering,
When they judged without skill, he was still hard of hearing;
When they talk'd of their Raphaels, Correggios, and stuff,
He shifted his trumpet,[19] and only took snuff.

[19] Sir Joshua Reynolds was so remarkably deaf as to be under the necessity of using an ear trumpet in company.

[On Ovid's *Epistles*]

Ovid's *Epistles, translated into* English *verse; with critical essays and notes. Being part of a poetical and oratorial lecture, read in the grammar-school of Ashford*, in the county of Kent; *and calculated to initiate youth in the first rudiments of taste. By* St. Barrett, *A.M. master of the said school. 8vo. Price 3s. 6d.* Richardson.

The praise which is every day lavished upon Virgil, Horace, or Ovid, is often no more than an indirect method the critic takes to compliment his own discernment. Their works have long been considered as models of beauty; to praise them now is only to shew the conformity of our taste to theirs: it tends not to advance their reputation, but to promote our own. Let us then dismiss, for the present, the pedantry of panegyric, Ovid needs it not, and we are not disposed to turn encomiasts on ourselves.

It will be sufficient to observe, that the multitude of translators which have attempted this poet, serves to evince the number of his admirers; and their indifferent success, the difficulty of equalling his elegance or his ease.

Dryden ever poor, and ever willing to be obliged, solicited the assistance of his friends for a translation of these epistles. It was not the first time his miseries obliged him to call in happier bards to his aid; and to permit such to quarter their fleeting performances on the lasting merit of his name. This eleemosinary translation, as might well be expected, was extremely unequal, frequently unjust to the poet's meaning, almost always so to his fame. It was published without notes; for it was not at that time customary to swell every performance of this nature with comment and scholia. The reader did not then chuse to have the current of his passions interrupted, his attention every moment called off from pleasure only, to be informed why he was so pleased. It was not then thought necessary to lessen surprize by anticipation, and, like some spectators we have met at the playhouse, to take off our attention from the performance, by telling, in our ear, what will follow next.

77

Since this united effort Ovid, as if born to misfortune, has undergone successive metamorphoses, being sometimes transposed by school-masters unacquainted with English, and sometimes transversed by ladies who knew no Latin: thus he has alternately worn the dress of a pedant or a rake; either crawling in humble prose, or having his hints explained into unbashful meaning. Schoolmasters, who knew all that was in him, except his graces, give the names of places and towns at full length, and he moves along stiffly in their literal versions, as the man who, as we are told, in the Philosophical Transactions, was afflicted with an universal anchylosis. His female imitators, on the other hand, regard the dear creature only as a lover, express the delicacy of his passion by the ardor of their own; and if now and then he is found to grow a little too warm, and perhaps to express himself a little indelicately, it must be imputed to the more poignant sensations of his fair admirers. In a word, we have seen him stripped of all his beauties in the versions of Stirling and Clark, and talk like a debauchee in that of Mrs — ; but the sex should ever be sacred from criticism; perhaps the ladies have a right to describe raptures, which none but themselves can bestow.

A poet, like Ovid, whose greatest beauty lies rather in expression than sentiment, must be necessarily difficult to translate. A fine sentiment may be conveyed several different ways, without impairing its vigour; but a sentence delicately expressed, will scarcely admit the least variation without losing beauty. The performance before us will serve to convince the public, that Ovid is more easily admired than imitated. The translator, in his notes, shews an ardent zeal for the reputation of his poet. It is possible too he may have felt his beauties, however he does not seem possessed of the happy art of giving his feelings expression. If a kindred spirit, as we have often been told, must animate the translator, we fear the claims of Mr Barrett will never receive a sanction in the heraldry of Parnassus.

His intentions, even envy must own, are laudable; nothing less than to instruct boys, schoolmasters, grown gentlemen, the public, *in the principles of taste* (to use his own expression) both by precept and by example. His manner it seems is, 'to read a course of poetical lectures to his pupils one night in the week; which, beginning with this author, running thro' select pieces of our own, as well as the Latin and Greek writers, and ending with Longinus, contributes *no little* towards forming their taste.' *No little*, reader, observe that, from a person so perfectly master of the force of his own language: what may not be expected from his comments on the beauties of another?

But, in order to shew in what manner he has executed these intentions, it is proper he should first march in review as a poet. We shall select the first epistle that offers, which is that from Penelope to Ulysses, observing before-hand, that the whole translation is a most convincing instance, that English words may be placed in Latin order, without being *wholly* unintelligible. Such forced transpositions serve at once to give an idea of the translator's learning, and of difficulties surmounted.

> *'Penelope* to *Ulysses.*
> This, still your wife, my ling'ring lord! I send:
> Yet be your answer personal, not penn'd.'

These lines seem happily imitated from Taylor, the water-poet, who has it thus:

> 'To thee, dear Ursula, these lines I send,
> Not with my hand but with my heart they're penn'd.'

But not to make a pause in the reader's pleasure, we proceed:

> 'Sunk now is Troy, the curse of Grecian dames!
> (Her king, her all, a worthless prize!) in flames.
> O had by storms (his fleet to Sparta bound)
> Th' adult'rer perish'd in the *mad profound!'*

Here seems some obscurity in the translation: we are at a loss to know what is meant by the *mad profound*. It can certainly mean neither Bedlam nor Fleet-Ditch; for tho' the epithet *mad* might agree with one, or *profound* with the other, yet when united they seem incompatible with either. The *profound* has frequently been used to signify bad verses; and poets are sometimes said to be *mad:* who knows but Penelope wishes that Paris might have died in the very act of rhyming; and as he was a shepherd, it is not improbable to suppose but that he was a poet also.

> 'Cold in a widow'd bed I ne'er had lay,
> Nor chid with weary eyes the ling'ring day.'

Lay, for *lain,* by the figure ginglimus. Our translator makes frequent use of this figure.

> 'Nor the protracted nuptials to avoid,
> By night unravell'd what the day employ'd.
>
> When have not fancied dangers broke my rest?
> Love, tim'rous passion! rends the anxious breast.
> In thought I saw you (each fierce Trojan's aim)
> Pale at the mention of bold Hector's name!'

Ovid makes Penelope shudder at the name of Hector. Our translator, with great propriety, transfers the fright from Penelope to Ulysses himself: it is he who grows pale at the name of Hector, and well indeed he might; for Hector is represented by Ovid, somewhere else, as a terrible fellow, and Ulysses as little better than a poltroon.

> 'Whose spear when brave Antilochus embru'd,
> By the dire news awoke, my fear renew'd.
> Clad in dissembled arms Patroclus died:
> And, "Oh the fate of stratagem!" I cried.
> Tlepolemus, beneath the Lycian dart,
> His breath resign'd, and rous'd afresh my smart.
> Thus, when each Grecian press'd the bloody field,
> Cold icy horrors my fond bosom chill'd.'

Here we may observe how epithets tend to strengthen the force of expression. First, her horrors are cold, and so far Ovid seems to think also; but the translator adds, from himself, the epithet icy, to shew that they are still colder: a fine climax of frigidity!

80

'But heaven indulgent to my chaste desire,
Has wrapp'd (my husband safe) proud Troy in fire.'

The reader may have already observed one or two instances
of our translator's skill, in parenthetically clapping one sentence
within another. This contributes not a little to obscurity; and
obscurity, we all know, is nearly allied to admiration. Thus, when
the reader begins a sentence which he finds pregnant with
another, which still teems with a third, and so on, he feels the
same surprize which a countryman does at Bartholomew-fair.
Hocus shews a bag, in appearance empty; slap, and out come a
dozen new-laid eggs; slap again, and the number is doubled: but
what is his amazement, when it swells with the hen that laid
them!

'The Grecian chiefs return, each altar shines,
And spoils of Asia grace our native shrines.
Gifts, for their lords restor'd, the matrons bring;
They Trojan fates o'ercome, triumphant sing;
Old men and trembling maids admire the songs,
And wives hang, list'ning, on their husbands' *tongues*.'

Critics have expatiated, in raptures, on the delicate use the
ancients have made of the verb *pendere*. Virgil's goats are described
as hanging on the mountain-side, the eyes of a lady hang on the
looks of her lover. Ovid has increased the force of the metaphor,
and describes the wife as hanging on the lips of her husband.
Our translator has gone still farther, and described the lady as
pendent from his tongue. – A fine picture!

'Now, drawn in wine, fierce battles meet their eyes,
And Ilion's tow'rs in miniature arise:
"There stretch'd Sigean plains, here Simoïs flow'd:
And there old Priam's lofty palace stood.
Here Peleus' son encamp'd, Ulysses there;
Here Hector's corpse distain'd the rapid car."
Of this the Pylian sage, in quest of thee
Embark'd, your son inform'd; his mother he.'

81

If we were permitted to offer a correction upon the two last lines, we would translate them into plain English thus, still preserving the rhyme entire.

> The Pylian sage inform'd your son embark'd in quest of thee,
> Of this, and he his mother, that is me.   [. . .]

>   'Three, helpless three! are here; a wife not strong,
>   A sire too aged, and a son too young,
>   He late, *by fraud*, imbark'd for Pylos' shore,
>   *Nigh from* my arms for ever had been tore.'

These two lines are replete with beauty; *nigh*, which implies approximation; and *from* which implies distance, are, to use our translator's expressions, drawn as it were up in line of battle. *Tore*, is put for *torn*, that is, torn by fraud from her arms; not that her son played truant and embarked by fraud, as a reader who does not understand Latin might be apt to fancy.

>   'Heaven grant the youth survive each parent's date,
>   And no cross chance reverse the course of fate.
>   Your nurse and herdsman join this wish of mine,
>   And the just keeper of your bristly swine.'

Our translator observes in a note, that 'the simplicity expressed in these lines is so far from being a blemish, that it is, in fact, a very great beauty: and the modern critic, who is offended with the mention of a *stye*, however he may pride himself upon his false delicacy, is either too short-sighted to penetrate into real nature, or has a stomach too nice to digest the noblest reliques of antiquity.' He means, no doubt, to digest an hog-stye; but, antiquity apart, we doubt if even Powell the fire-eater, himself, could bring his appetite to relish so unsavoury a repast.

>   'By age your sire disarm'd, and wasting woes,
>   The helm resigns, amidst surrounding foes.
>   This may your son resume (when years allow)
>   But oh! a father's aid is wanted now.

82

Nor have I strength his title to maintain,
Haste then, our only refuge, o'er the main.

'A son, and long may heaven the blessing grant,
You have, whose years a sire's instructions want.
Think how Laërtes drags an age of woes,
In hope that you his dying eyes may close.
And I, left youthful in my early bloom,
Shall aged seem; how soon soe'er you come.'

But let not the reader imagine we can find pleasure in thus exposing absurdities, which are too ludicrous for serious reproof. While we censure as critics, we feel as men, and could sincerely wish that those, whose greatest sin is, perhaps, the venial one of writing bad verses, would regard their failure in this respect as we do, not as faults but foibles; they may be good and useful members of society, without being poets. The regions of taste can be travelled only by a few, and even those often find indifferent accommodation by the way. Let such as have not got a passport from nature be content with happiness, and leave the poet the unrivalled possession of his misery, his garret, and his fame.

We have of late seen the republic of letters crowded with some, who have no other pretensions to applause but industry, who have no other merit but that of reading many books, and making long quotations; these we have heard extolled by sympathetic dunces, and have seen them carry off the rewards of genius; while others, who should have been born in better days, felt all the wants of poverty, and the agonies of contempt. Who then that has a regard for the public, for the literary honours of our country, for the figure we shall one day make among posterity, that would not chuse to see such humbled as are possessed only of talents that might have made good coblers, had fortune turn'd them to trade. Should such prevail, the real interests of learning must be in a reciprocal proportion to the power they possess. Let it be then the character of our periodical endeavours, and hitherto we flatter ourselves it has ever been, not to permit an ostentation of learning pass for merit, nor to give a pedant quarter upon the score of his industry alone, even tho' he took refuge behind Arabic, or powdered his hair with hieroglyphics. Authors thus censured may accuse our judgment or our reading, if they please, but our own hearts will acquit us of envy or ill-nature, since we reprove only with a desire to reform.

But we had almost forgot, that our translator is to be considered as a critic as well as a poet; and in this department he seems also equally unsuccessful with the former. Criticism at present is different from what it was upon the revival of taste in Europe; all its rules are now well known; the only art at present is, to exhibit them in such lights, as contribute to keep the attention alive and excite a favourable audience. It must borrow graces from eloquence, and please while it aims at instruction: but instead of this we have a combination of trite observations, delivered in a stile, in which those who are disposed to make war upon words, will find endless opportunities of triumph.

He is sometimes hypercritical. Thus, p.9. 'Pope, in his excellent Essay on Criticism (as will, in its place, when you come to be lectured upon it, at full be explained) terms this making the sound an echo to the sense. But I apprehend that definition takes in but a part, for the best ancient poets excelled, in thus painting to the eye as well as to the ear. Virgil, describing his house-wife preparing her wine, exhibits the act of the fire to the eye.

> "Aut dulcis musti Vulcano decoquit humorem,
> Et foliis undam trepidi dispumat aheni."

For the line (if I may be allowed the expression) boils over; and, in order to reduce it to its proper bounds, you must, with her, skim off the redundant syllable.' These are beauties which, doubtless the reader is displeased he cannot discern.

Sometimes confused: 'There is a *deal* of artful and concealed satire in what Oenone throws out against Helen; and to speak truth, there was fair scope for it, and it might naturally be expected. Her chief design was to render his new mistress suspected of meretricious arts, and make him apprehensive that she would hereafter be as ready to leave him for some new gallant,

84

as she had before, perfidiously to her lawful husband, followed him.'

Sometimes contradictory: thus, p.3. 'Stile, (says he) is used by some writers, as synonimous with diction; yet in my opinion, it has rather a complex sense, including both sentiment and diction.' Oppose to this, p.135. 'As to concord, and even stile, they are acquirable by most youth in due time, and by many with ease; but the art of thinking properly, and chusing the best sentiments on every subject, is what comes later.'

And sometimes he is guilty of false criticism: as when he says, Ovid's chief excellence lies in description. Description was the rock on which he always split; *Nescivit quod bene cessit relinquere*, as Seneca says of him; when once he embarks in description, he most commonly tires us before he has done with it. But to tire no longer the reader, or the translator, with extended censure; as a critic, this gentleman seems to have drawn his knowledge from the remarks of others, and not his own reflection; as a translator, he understands the language of Ovid, but not his beauties; and tho' he may be an excellent school-master, he has, however, no pretensions to taste.

From *An Enquiry into the Present State of Polite Learning in Europe*

CHAPTER X
Of the encouragement of learning.

There is nothing authors are more apt to lament, than want of encouragement from the age. Whatever their differences in other respects may be, they are all ready to unite in this complaint, and each indirectly offers himself as an instance of the truth of his assertion.

The beneficed divine, whose wants are only imaginary, expostulates as bitterly as the poorest author, that ever snuffed his candle with finger and thumb. Should interest or good fortune, advance the divine to a bishopric, or the poor son of Parnassus into that place where the other has resign'd; both are authors no longer, the one goes to prayers once a day, kneels upon cushions of velvet, and thanks gracious heaven for having made the circumstances of all mankind so extremely happy; the other battens on all the delicacies of life, enjoys his wife and his easy chair, and sometimes, for the sake of conversation, deplores the luxury of these degenerate days.

All encouragements to merit are misapplied, which make the author too rich to continue his profession. There can be nothing more just than the old observation, that authors, like running horses, should be fed but not fattened. If we would continue them in our service, we should reward them with a little money and a great deal of praise, still keeping their avarice subservient to their ambition. Not that I think a writer incapable of filling an employment with dignity, I would only insinuate, that when made a bishop or statesman, he will continue to please us as a writer no longer. As to resume a former allusion, the running horse, when fattened, will still be fit for very useful purposes, though unqualified for a courser.

No nation gives greater encouragements to learning than we do; yet, at the same time, none are so injudicious in the application. We seem to confer them with the same view, that statesmen have been known to grant employments at court, rather as bribes to silence, than incentives to emulation.

Upon this principle, all our magnificent endowments of colleges are erroneous, and, at best, more frequently enrich the prudent than reward the ingenious. A lad whose passions are not strong enough in youth to mislead him from that path of science, which his tutors, and not his inclinations, have chalked out, by four or five years perseverance, may probably obtain every advantage and honour his college can bestow. I forget whether the simile has been used before but I would compare the man, whose youth has been thus passed in the tranquility of dispassionate prudence, to liquors which never ferment, and consequently, continue always muddy. Passions may raise a commotion in the youthful breast, but they disturb only to refine it. However this be, mean talents are often rewarded in colleges, with an easy subsistence. The candidates for preferments of this kind, often regard their admission as a patent for future laziness; so that a life begun in studious labour, is often continued in luxurious affluence.

Among the universities abroad, I have ever observed their riches and their learning in a reciprocal proportion, their stupidity and pride increasing with their opulence. Happening once in conversation with Gaubius of Leyden,* to mention the college of Edinburgh, he began by complaining that all the English students, which formerly came to his university, now went intirely there; and the fact surprized him more, as Leyden was now as well as ever furnished with masters excellent in their respective professions. He concluded by asking, if the professors of Edinburgh were rich. I reply'd, that the salary of a professor there seldom amounted to more than thirty pounds a year. Poor men, says he, I heartily wish they were better provided for, until they become rich, we can have no expectation of English students at Leyden.

Premiums also, proposed for literary excellence, when given as encouragements to boys may be useful, but when designed as rewards to men, are certainly misapplied. We have seldom seen a performance of any great merit, in consequence of rewards proposed in this manner. Who has ever observed a writer of any eminence, a candidate in so precarious a contest? The man who knows the real value of his own genius, will no more venture it upon an uncertainty, than he who knows the true use of a guinea, will stake it with a sharper by throwing a main.

Every encouragement given to stupidity, when known to be such, is also a negative insult upon genius. This appears in nothing more evident, than the undistinguished success of those who sollicit subscriptions. When first brought into fashion, subscriptions were conferred upon the ingenious alone, or those who were reputed as such. But at present, we see them made a resource of indigence, and requested not as rewards of merit, but as a relief of distress. If tradesmen happen to want skill in conducting their own business, yet they are able to write a book; if mechanics want money, or ladies shame, they write books and solicit subscriptions. Scarce a morning passes, that proposals of this nature are not thrust into the half-opening doors of the rich, with, perhaps, a paltry petition, shewing the author's wants, but not his merits. I would not willingly prevent that pity which is due to indigence, but while the streams of liberality are thus diffused, they must in the end become proportionably shallow.

What then are the proper encouragements of genius? I answer, subsistence and respect, for these are rewards congenial to its nature. Every animal has an aliment peculiarly suited to its constitution. The heavy ox seeks nourishment from the earth; the light cameleon has been supposed to exist on air; a sparer diet even than this, will satisfy the man of true genius, for he makes a luxurious banquet on empty applause. It is this alone, which has inspired all that ever was truly great and noble among us. It is, as Cicero finely calls it the eccho of virtue. Avarice is the passion of inferior natures; money the pay of the common herd. The author who draws his quill merely to take a purse, no more deserves success than he who presents a pistol.

When the link between patronage and learning was entire, then all who deserved fame were in a capacity of attaining it. When the great Somers was at the helm, patronage was fashionable among our nobility. The middle ranks of mankind, who generally imitate the Great, then followed their example; and applauded from fashion, if not from feeling. I have heard an old poet [Edward Young] of that glorious age say, that a dinner with his lordship, has procured him invitations for the whole week following: that an airing in his patron's chariot, has supplied him with a citizen's coach on every future occasion. For who would not be proud to entertain a man who kept so much good company?

But this link now seems entirely broken. Since the days of a certain prime minister [Robert Walpole] of inglorious memory, the learned have been kept pretty much at a distance. A jockey, or a laced player, supplies the place of the scholar, poet, or the man of virtue. Those conversations, once the result of wisdom, wit, and innocence, are now turned to humbler topics, little more being expected from a companion than a laced coat, a pliant bow, and an immoderate friendship for – a well served table.

Wit, when neglected by the great, is generally despised by the vulgar. Those who are unacquainted with the world, are apt to fancy the man of wit, as leading a very agreeable life. They conclude, perhaps, that he is attended to with silent admiration, and dictates to the rest of mankind, with all the eloquence of conscious superiority. Very different is his present situation. He is called an author, and all know that an author is a thing only to be laughed at. His person, not his jest, becomes the mirth of the company. At his approach, the most fat unthinking face, brightens into malicious meaning. Even aldermen laugh, and revenge on him, the ridicule which was lavish'd on their forefathers.

> Etiam victis redit in præcordia virtus,
> Victoresque cadunt.*

It is indeed a reflection somewhat mortifying to the author, who breaks his ranks, and singles out for public favour to think that he must combat contempt, before he can arrive at glory. That he must expect to have all the fools of society united against him, before he can hope for the applause of the judicious. For this, however, he must prepare beforehand; as those who have no idea of the difficulty of his employment, will be apt to regard his inactivity as idleness, and not having a notion of the pangs of uncomplying thought in themselves, it is not to be expected they should have any desire of rewarding by respecting them in others.   [. . .]

Yet it were well, if none but the duncers of society, were combined to render the profession of an author ridiculous or unhappy. Men of the first eminence are often found to indulge this illiberal vein of raillery. Two contending writers often by the opposition of their wit, render their profession contemptible in the eyes of ignorants, who should have been taught to admire. Whatever the reader may think of himself, it is at least two to one, but he is a greater blockhead than the most scribbling dunce he affects to despise.

The poet's poverty is a standing topic of contempt. His writing for bread is an unpardonable offence. Perhaps, of all mankind, an author, in these times, is used most hardly. We keep him poor, and yet revile his poverty. Like angry parents, who correct their children till they cry, and then correct them for crying, we reproach him for living by his wit, and yet allow him no other means to live.

His taking refuge in garrets and cellars, and living among vermin, have, of late been violently objected to him, and that by men, who I dare hope, are more apt to pity than insult his distress. Is poverty the writer's fault? No doubt, he knows how to prefer a bottle of champaign, to the nectar of the neighbouring alehouse, or a venison pasty to a plate of potatoes. Want of delicacy is not in him, but in us, who deny him the opportunity of making an elegant choice.

Wit certainly is the property of those who have it, nor should we be displeased if it is the only property a man sometimes has. We must not under-rate him who uses it for subsistence, and flies from the ingratitude of the age, even to a bookseller for redress. If the profession of an author is to be laughed at by stupids, it is certainly better sure to be contemptibly rich, than contemptibly poor. For all the wit that ever adorned the human mind, will at present no more shield the author's poverty from ridicule, than his high topped gloves conceal the unavoidable omissions of his laundress.

To be more serious, new fashions, follies, and vices, make new monitors necessary in every age. An author may be considered as a merciful substitute to the legislature; he acts not by punishing crimes, but preventing them; however virtuous the present age, there may be still growing employment for ridicule, or reproof,

90

for persuasion, or satire. If the author be, therefore, still so necessary among us, let us treat him with proper consideration, as a child of the public, not a rent-charge on the community. And, indeed, a *child* of the public he is in all respects; for while so well able to direct others, how incapable is he frequently found of guiding himself. His simplicity exposes him to all the insidious approaches of cunning, his sensibility to the slightest invasions of contempt. Though possessed of fortitude to stand unmoved the expected bursts of an earthquake, yet of feelings so exquisitely poignant, as to agonize under the slightest disappointment. Broken rest, tasteless meals, and causeless anxiety, shorten his life, or render it unfit for active employment; prolonged vigils, and intense application still farther contract his span, and make his time glide insensibly away. Let us not then aggravate those natural inconveniences by neglect; we have had sufficient instances of this kind already. Sale, Savage, Amherst, More* will suffice for one age at least. But they are dead, and their sorrows are over. The neglected author of the Persian eclogues, which, however inaccurate, excel any in our language, is still alive. Happy, if *insensible* of our neglect, not *raging* at our ingratitude. It is enough, that the age has already yielded instances of men pressing foremost in the lists of fame, and worthy of better times, schooled by continued adversity into an hatred of their kind, flying from thought to drunkenness, yielding to the united pressure of labour, penury, and sorrow, sinking unheeded, without one friend to drop a tear on their unattended obsequies, and indebted to charity for a grave among the dregs of mankind.

The author, when unpatronized by the Great, has naturally recourse to the bookseller. There cannot be, perhaps, imagined a combination more prejudicial to taste than this. It is the interest of the one to allow as little for writing, and of the other to write as much, as possible; accordingly, tedious compilations, and periodical magazines, are the result of their joint endeavours. In these circumstances, the author bids adieu to fame, writes for bread, and for that only. Imagination is seldom called in; he sits down to address the venal muse with the most phlegmatic apathy;

and, as we are told of the Russian, courts his mistress by falling asleep in her lap. His reputation never spreads in a wider circle than that of the trade, who generally value him, not for the fineness of his compositions, but the quantity he works off in a given time.

A long habitude of writing for bread, thus turns the ambition of every author at last into avarice. He finds, that he has wrote many years, that the public are scarcely acquainted even with his name; he despairs of applause, and turns to profit, which invites him. He finds that money procures all those advantages, that respect, and that ease, which he vainly expected of fame. Thus the man, who under the protection of the Great, might have done honour to humanity, when only patronized by the bookseller, becomes a thing little superior to the fellow who works at the press.

Sint Mæcenates, non deerunt, Flacce, Marones.*

CHAPTER XI
Upon Criticism.

But there are still some men, whom fortune has blessed with affluence, to whom the muse pays her morning visit, not like a creditor, but a friend: to this happy few, who have leisure to polish what they write, and liberty to chuse their own subjects, I would direct my advice, which consists in a few words: *Write what you think, regardless of the critics.* To persuade to this, was the chief design of this essay. To break, or at least to loosen those bonds, first put on by caprice, and afterwards drawn hard by fashion, is my wish. I have assumed the critic only to dissuade from criticism.

There is scarce an error of which our present writers are guilty, that does not arise from this source. From this proceeds the affected obscurity of our odes, the tuneless flow of our blank verse, the pompous epithet, laboured diction, and every other deviation from common sense, which procures the poet the applause of the connoisseur; he is praised by all, read by a few, and soon forgotten.

There never was an unbeaten path trodden by the poet, that the critic did not endeavour to reclaim him, by calling his attempt innovation. This might be instanced in Dante, who first followed nature, and was persecuted by the critics as long as he lived. Thus novelty, one of the greatest beauties in poetry, must be avoided, or the connoisseur will be displeased. It is one of the chief privileges, however, of genius, to fly from the herd of imitators by some happy singularity; for should he stand still, his heavy pursuers will at length come up, and fairly dispute the victory.

The ingenious Mr Hogarth used to assert, that every one, except the connoisseur, was a judge of painting. The same may be asserted of writing; the public in general set the whole piece in the proper point of view; the critic lays his eye close to all its minutenesses, and condemns or approves in detail. And this may be the reason why so many writers at present, are apt to appeal from the tribunal of criticism to that of the people.

From a desire in the critic of grafting the spirit of ancient languages upon the English, has proceeded of late several disagreeable instances of pedantry. Among the number, I think we may reckon blank verse. Nothing but the greatest sublimity of subject can render such a measure pleasing; however, we now see it used upon the most trivial occasions; it has particularly found its way into our didactic poetry, and is likely to bring that species of composition into disrepute, for which the English are deservedly famous.

Those who are acquainted with writing, know that our language runs almost naturally into blank verse. The writers of our novels, romances, and all of this class, who have no notion of stile, naturally hobble into this unharmonious measure. If rhymes, therefore, be more difficult, for that very reason, I would have our poets write in rhyme. Such a restriction upon the thought of a good poet, often lifts and encreases the vehemence

93

of every sentiment; for fancy, like a fountain, plays highest by diminishing the aperture. But rhymes, it will be said, are a remnant of monkish stupidity, an innovation upon the poetry of the ancients. They are but indifferently acquainted with antiquity, who make the assertion. Rhymes are probably of older date than either the Greek or Latin dactyl and spondé. The Celtic, which is allowed to be the first language spoken in Europe, has ever preserved them, as we may find in the Edda of Iceland, and the Irish carrols still sung among the original inhabitants of that island. Olaus Wormius gives us some of the Teutonic poetry in this way; and Pantoppidan, bishop of Bergen, some of the Norwegian; in short, this jingle of sounds is almost natural to mankind, at least, it is so to our language, if we may judge from many unsuccessful attempts to throw it off.

I should not have employed so much time in opposing this erroneous innovation, if it were not apt to introduce another in its train: I mean, a disgusting solemnity of manner into our poetry; and, as the prose writer has been ever found to follow the poet, it must consequently banish in both, all that agreeable trifling, which, if I may so express it, often deceives us into instruction. Dry reasoning, and dull morality, have no force with the wild fantastic libertine. He must be met with smiles, and courted with the allurements of gaiety. He must be taught to believe, that he is in pursuit of pleasure, and surprized into reformation. The finest sentiment, and the most weighty truth, may put on a pleasing face, and it is even virtuous to jest when serious advice must be disgusting. But instead of this, the most trifling performance among us now, assumes all the didactic stiffness of wisdom. The most diminutive son of fame, or of famine, has his *we* and his *us*, his *firstlys* and his *secondlys* as methodical, as if bound in cow-hide, and closed with clasps of brass. Were these Monthly Reviews and Magazines frothy, pert, or absurd, they might find some pardon; but to be dull and dronish, is an encroachment on the prerogative of a folio.

These pamphlets should be considered as pills to purge melancholly; they should be made up in our splenetic climate, to be

94

taken as physic, and not so as to be used when we take it. Some such law should be enacted in the republic of letters, as we find take place in the house of commons. As no man there can shew his wisdom, unless first qualified by three hundred pounds a year, so none here should profess gravity, unless his work amounted to three hundred pages.

However, by the power of one single monosyllable, our critics have almost got the victory over humour amongst us. Does the poet paint the absurdities of the vulgar; then he is *low*: does he exaggerate the features of folly, to render it more thoroughly ridiculous, he is then very *low*. In short, they have proscribed the comic or satyrical muse from every walk but high life, which, though abounding in fools as well as the humblest station, is by no means so fruitful in absurdity. Among well-bred fools we may despise much, but have little to laugh at; nature seems to present us with an universal blank of silk, ribbands, smiles, and whispers; absurdity is the poet's game, and good breeding is the nice concealment of absurdities. The truth is, the critic generally mistakes humour for wit, which is a very different excellence. Wit raises human nature above its level; humour acts a contrary part, and equally depresses it. To expect exalted humour; is a contradiction in terms; and the critic, by demanding an impossibility from the comic poet, has, in effect, banished new comedy from the stage. But to put the same thought in a different light:

When an unexpected similitude in two objects strikes the imagination; in other words, when a thing is *wittily* expressed, all our pleasure turns into admiration of the artist, who had fancy enough to draw the picture. When a thing is *humourously* described, our burst of laughter proceeds from a very different cause; we compare the absurdity of the character represented with our own, and triumph in our conscious superiority. No natural defect can be a cause of laughter, because it is a misfortune to which ourselves are liable; a defect of this kind changes the passion to pity or horror; we only laugh at those instances of moral absurdity, to which we are conscious we ourselves are not liable. For instance, should I describe a man as wanting his nose, there is

95

no humour in this, as it is an accident to which human nature is subject, and may be any man's case: but should I represent this man without his nose, as extremely curious in the choice of his snuff-box, we here see him guilty of an absurdity of which we imagine it impossible for ourselves to be guilty, and therefore applaud our own good sense on the comparison. Thus, then, the pleasure we receive from wit, turns on the admiration of another; that we feel from humour, centers in the admiration of ourselves. The poet, therefore, must place the object he would have the subject of humour in a state of inferiority; in other words, the subject of humour must be low.

The solemnity worn by many of our modern writers is, I fear, often the mask of dulness; for certain it is, it seems to fit every author who pleases to put it on. By the complexion of many of our late publications, one might be apt to cry out with Cicero, *Civem mehercule non puto esse qui his temporibus ridere possit.* On my conscience, I believe we have all forgot to laugh in these days. Such writers probably make no distinction between what is praised, and what is pleasing; between those commendations which the reader pays his own discernment, and those which are the genuine result of his sensations.

As our gentlemen writers have it therefore so much in their power to lead the taste of the times, they may now part with the inflated stile that has for some years been looked upon as fine writing, and which every young writer is now obliged to adopt, if he chuses to be read. They may now dispense with loaded epithet, and dressing up of trifles with dignity. For to use an obvious instance, it is not those who make the greatest noise with their wares in the streets, that have the most to sell. Let us, instead of writing finely, try to write naturally. Not hunt after lofty expressions to deliver mean ideas; nor be for ever gaping, when we only mean to deliver a whisper.

From *The Bee:*
Being Essays on the Most Interesting Subjects

ON THE USE OF LANGUAGE

The manner in which most writers begin their treatises on the Use of Language, is generally thus: "Language has been granted to man, in order to discover his wants and necessities, so as to have them relieved by society. Whatever we desire, whatever we wish, it is but to cloath those desires or wishes in words, in order to fruition; the principal use of language, therefore, say they, is to express our wants, so as to receive a speedy redress."

Such an account as this may serve to satisfy grammarians and rhetoricians well enough, but men who know the world, maintain very contrary maxims; they hold, and I think with some shew of reason, they hold that he who best knows how to conceal his necessities and desires, is the most likely person to find redress, and that the true use of speech is not so much to express our wants as to conceal them.

When we reflect on the manner in which mankind generally confer their favours, we shall find that they who seem to want them least, are the very persons who most liberally share them. There is something so attractive in riches, that the large heap generally collects from the smaller; and the poor find as much pleasure in encreasing the enormous mass, as the miser, who owns it, sees happiness in its encrease. Nor is there in this any thing repugnant to the laws of true morality. Seneca himself allows, that in conferring benefits, the present should always be suited to the dignity of the receiver. Thus the rich receive large presents, and are thanked for accepting them. Men of middling stations are obliged to be content with presents something less, while the beggar, who may be truly said to want indeed, is well paid if a farthing rewards his warmest solicitations.

Every man who has seen the world, and has had his *ups and downs in life*, as the expression is, must have frequently experienced the truth of this doctrine, and must know that to have much, or to seem to have it, is the only way to have more. Ovid finely compares a man of broken fortune to a falling column; the lower it sinks, the greater weight it is obliged to sustain. Thus, when a man has no occasion to borrow, he finds numbers willing to lend him. Should he ask a friend to lend him an hundred pounds, it is possible, from the largeness of the demand, he may find credit for twenty; but should he humbly only sue for a trifle, it is two to one whether he might be trusted for two pence. A certain young fellow at George's, whenever he had occasion to ask his friend for a guinea, used to prelude his request as if he wanted two hundred, and talked so familiarly of large sums, that none could ever think he wanted a small one. The same gentleman, whenever he wanted credit for a new suit from his taylor, always made the proposal in laced cloaths; for he found by experience, that if he appeared shabby on these occasions, Mr Lynch had taken an oath against trusting; or what was every bit as bad, his foreman was out of the way, and would not be at home these two days.

There can be no inducement to reveal our wants, except to find pity, and by this means relief; but before a poor man opens his mind in such circumstances, he should first consider whether he is contented to lose the esteem of the person he solicits, and whether he is willing to give up friendship only to excite compassion. Pity and friendship are passions incompatible with each other, and it is impossible that both can reside in any breast for the smallest space, without impairing each other. Friendship is made up of esteem and pleasure; pity is composed of sorrow and contempt: the mind may for some time fluctuate between them, but it never can entertain both together.

Yet let it not be thought that I would exclude pity from the human mind. There is scarce any who are not in some degree possessed of this pleasing softness; but it is at best but a short-lived passion, and seldom affords distress more than transitory assistance: With some it scarce lasts from the first impulse till the hand can be put into the pocket; with others it may continue for twice that space, and on some of extraordinary sensibility, I have seen it operate for half an hour. But, however, last as it will, it generally produces but beggarly effects; and where, from this motive we give an halfpenny, from others we give always pound. In great distress we sometimes, it is true, feel the influence of tenderness strongly; when the same distress solicits a second time, we then feel with diminished sensibility, but like the repetition of an eccho, every new impulse becomes weaker, till at last our sensations lose every mixture of sorrow, and degenerate into downright contempt.

Jack Spindle and I were old acquaintance; but he's gone. Jack was bred in a compting-house, and his father dying just as he was out of his time, left him an handsome fortune, and many friends to advise with. The restraint in which he had been brought up, had thrown a gloom upon his temper, which some regarded as an habitual prudence, and from such considerations, he had every day repeated offers of friendship. Those who had money, were ready to offer him their assistance that way; and they who had daughters, frequently, in the warmth of affection, advised him to marry. Jack, however, was in good circumstances; he wanted neither money, friends, nor a wife, and therefore modestly declined their proposals.

Some errors in the management of his affairs, and several losses in trade, soon brought Jack to a different way of thinking; and he at last thought it his best way to let his friends know that their offers were at length acceptable. His first address was therefore to a scrivener, who had formerly made him frequent offers of money and friendship, at a time when, perhaps, he knew those offers would have been refused.

Jack, therefore, thought he might use his old friend without any ceremony, and as a man confident of not being refused, requested the use of an hundred guineas for a few days, as he just then had an occasion for money. "And pray, Mr Spindle, replied the scrivener, do you want all this money?" "Want it, Sir, says the other, if I did not want it, I should not have asked it." "I am sorry for that, says the friend; for those who want money when they come to borrow, will want money when they should come to pay. To say the truth, Mr Spindle, money is money now-a-days. I believe it is all sunk in the bottom of the sea, for my part; and he that has got a little, is a fool if he does not keep what he has got."

Not quite disconcerted by this refusal, our adventurer was resolved to apply to another, whom he knew to be the very best friend he had in the world. The gentleman whom he now addressed, received his proposal with all the affability that could be expected from generous friendship. "Let me see, you want an hundred guineas; and pray, dear Jack, would not fifty answer?" *"If you have but fifty to spare, Sir, I must be contented."* "Fifty to spare, I do not say that, for I believe I have but twenty about me." *"Then I must borrow the other thirty from some other friend."* "And pray, replied the friend, would it not be the best way to borrow the whole money from that other friend, and then one note will serve for all, you know. Lord, Mr Spindle, make no ceremony with me at any time; you know I'm your friend, and when you chuse a bit of dinner or so. – You, Tom, see the gentleman down. You won't forget to dine with us now and then. Your very humble servant."

Distressed, but not discouraged at this treatment, he was at last resolved to find that assistance from love, which he could not have from friendship. Miss Jenny Dismal had a fortune in her own hands, and she had already made all the advances that her sex's modesty would permit. He made his proposal, therefore with confidence, but soon perceived, *No bankrupt ever found the fair one kind.* Miss Jenny and Master Billy Galloon were lately fallen deeply in love with each other, and the whole neighbourhood thought it would soon be a match.

Every day now began to strip Jack of his former finery; his cloaths flew piece by piece to the pawnbroker's, and he seemed at length equipped in the genuine mourning of antiquity. But still he thought himself secure from starving, the numberless invitations he had received to dine, even after his losses, were yet unanswered; he was therefore now resolved to accept of a dinner because he wanted one; and in this manner he actually

100

lived among his friends a whole week without being openly affronted. The last place I saw poor Jack was at the Rev. Dr. Gosling's. He had, as he fancied, just nicked the time, for he came in as the cloth was laying. He took a chair without being desired, and talked for some time without being attended to. He assured the company, that nothing procured so good an appetite as a walk to White Conduit-house, where he had been that morning. He looked at the table-cloth, and praised the figure of the damask; talked of a feast where he had been the day before, but that the venison was over done. All this, however, procured the poor creature no invitation, and he was not yet sufficiently hardened to stay without being asked; wherefore, finding the gentleman of the house insensible to all his fetches, he thought proper, at last, to retire, and mend his appetite by a walk in the Park.

You then, O ye beggars of my acquaintance, whether in rags or lace; whether in Kent-street or the Mall; whether at the Smyrna or St. Giles's, might I advise as a friend, never seem in want of the favour which you solicit. Apply to every passion but pity, for redress. You may find relief from vanity, from self-interest, or from avarice, but seldom from compassion. The very eloquence of a poor man is disgusting; and that mouth which is opened even for flattery, is seldom expected to close without a petition.

If then you would ward off the gripe of poverty, pretend to be a stranger to her, and she will at least use you with ceremony. Hear not my advice, but that of Offellus. If you be caught dining upon a halfpenny porrenger of pease soup and potatoes, praise the wholesomeness of your frugal repast. You may observe, that Dr. Cheyne has prescribed pease broth for the gravel, hint that you are not one of those who are always making a god of your belly. If you are obliged to wear a flimsy stuff in the midst of winter, be the first to remark that stuffs are very much worn at Paris. If there be found some irreparable defects in any part of your equipage, which cannot be concealed by all the arts of sitting cross-legged, coaxing, or derning, say, that neither you nor Sampson Gideon were ever very fond of dress. Or if you be a philosopher, hint that Plato and Seneca are the taylors you choose to employ; assure the company that men ought to be content with a bare covering, since what is now the pride of some, was formerly our shame. Horace will give you a Latin sentence fit for the occasion,

Toga quæ defendere frigus quamvis crassa queat.*

In short, however caught, do not give up, but ascribe to the frugality of your disposition what others might be apt to attribute to the narrowness of your circumstances, and appear rather to be a miser than a beggar. To be poor, and to seem poor, is a certain method never to rise. Pride in the great is hateful, in the wise it is ridiculous; *beggarly pride* is the only sort of vanity I can excuse.

MISCELLANEOUS

Were I to measure the merit of my present undertaking by its success, or the rapidity of its sale, I might be led to form conclusions by no means favourable to the pride of an author. Should I estimate my fame by its extent, every Newspaper and every Magazine would leave me far behind. Their fame is diffused in a very wide circle, that of some as far as Islington, and some yet farther still; while mine, I sincerely believe, has hardly travelled beyond the sound of Bow-bell; and while the works of others fly like unpinioned swans, I find my own move as heavily as a new-plucked goose.

Still, however, I have as much pride as they who have ten times as many readers. It is impossible to repeat all the agreeable delusions in which a disappointed author is apt to find comfort. I conclude, that what my reputation wants in extent, is made up by its solidity. *Minus juvat Gloria lata quam magna.** I have great satisfaction in considering the delicacy and discernment of those readers I have, and in ascribing my want of popularity to the ignorance or inattention of those I have not. All the world may forsake an author, but vanity will never forsake him.

Yet notwithstanding so sincere a confession, I was once induced to shew my indignation against the public, by discontinuing my endeavours to please; and was bravely resolved, like Raleigh, to vex them, by burning my manuscript in a passion. Upon recollection, however, I considered what set or body of people would be displeased at my rashness. The sun, after so sad an accident, might shine next morning as bright as usual; men might laugh and sing the next day, and transact business as before, and not a single creature feel any regret but myself.

I reflected upon the story of a minister, who, in the reign of Charles II, upon a certain occasion, resigned all his posts, and retired into the country in a fit of resentment. But as he had not given the world entirely up with his ambition, he sent a messenger to town, to see how the courtiers would bear his resignation. Upon the messenger's return, he was asked whether there appeared any commotions at court? To which he replied, There were very great ones. "Ay, says the minister, I knew my friends would make a bustle; all petitioning the king for my restoration, I presume." "No, Sir, replied the messenger, they are only petitioning his majesty to be put in your place." In the same manner, should I retire in indignation, instead of having Apollo in mourning, or the Muses in a fit of the spleen; instead of having the learned world apostrophising at my untimely decease, perhaps all Grub-street might laugh at my fall, and self-approving dignity might never be able to shield me from ridicule. In short, I am resolved to write on, if it were only to spite them. If the present generation will not hear my voice, hearken, O posterity, to you I call, and from you I expect redress! What rapture will it not give to have the Scaligers, Daciers, and Warburtons of future times commenting with admiration upon every line I now write, working away those ignorant creatures who offer to arraign my merit with all the virulence of learned reproach. Ay, my friends, let them feel it; call names; never spare them; they deserve it all, and ten times more. I have been told of a critic, who was crucified,

103

at the command of another, to the reputation of Homer. That, no doubt, was more than poetical justice, and I shall be perfectly content if those who criticise me are only clapped in the pillory, kept fifteen days upon bread and water, and obliged to run the gantlope through Pater-noster Row. The truth is, I can expect happiness from posterity either way. If I write ill, happy in being forgotten; if well, happy in being remembered with respect.

Yet, considering things in a prudential light, perhaps I was mistaken in designing my paper as an agreeable relaxation to the studious, or an help to conversation among the gay; instead of addressing it to such, I should have written down to the taste and apprehension of the many, and sought for reputation on the broad road. Literary fame I now find like religious, generally begins among the vulgar. As for the polite, they are so very polite, as never to applaud upon any account. One of these, with a face screwed up into affectation, tells you, that fools may *admire*, but men of sense only *approve*. Thus, lest he should rise into rapture at any thing new, he keeps down every passion but pride and self-importance; approves with phlegm, and the poor author is damned in the taking a pinch of snuff. Another has written a book himself, and being condemned for a dunce, he turns a sort of king's evidence in criticism, and now becomes the terror of every offender. A third, possessed of full-grown reputation, shades off every beam of favour from those who endeavour to grow beneath him, and keeps down that merit, which, but for his influence, might rise into equal eminence. While others, still worse, peruse old books for their amusement, and new books only to condemn; so that the public seem heartily sick of all but the business of the day, and read every thing new with as little attention as they examine the faces of the passing crowd.

From these considerations I was once determined to throw off all connexions with taste, and fairly address my countrymen in the same engaging style and manner with other periodical pamphlets, much more in vogue than probably mine shall ever be. To effect this, I had thoughts of changing the title into that of the ROYAL BEE, the ANTI-GALLICAN BEE, or the BEE'S MAGAZINE. I had laid in a proper stock of popular topicks, such as encomiums on the king of Prussia, invectives against the queen of Hungary and the French, the necessity of a militia, our undoubted sovereignty of the seas, reflections upon the present state of affairs, a dissertation upon liberty, some seasonable thoughts upon the intended bridge of Blackfriars, and an address to Britons. The history of an old woman, whose teeth grew three inches long, an ode upon our victories, a rebus, an acrostic upon Miss Peggy P. and a journal of the weather. All this, together with four extraordinary pages of *letter press*, a beautiful map of England, and two prints curiously coloured from nature, I fancied might touch their very souls. I was actually beginning an address to the people, when my pride at last overcame my prudence, and determined me to endeavour to please by the goodness of my entertainment, rather than by the magnificence of my sign.

The Spectator, and many succeeding essayists, frequently inform us of the numerous compliments paid them in the course of their lucubrations; of the frequent encouragements they met to inspire them with ardour, and increase their eagerness to please. I have received *my letters* as well as they; but alas! not congratulatory ones; not assuring me of success and favour; but pregnant with bodings that might shake even fortitude itself.

One gentleman assures me, he intends to throw away no more three-pences in purchasing the BEE; and what is still more dismal, he will not recommend me as a poor author wanting encouragement to his neighbourhood, which it seems is very numerous. Were my soul set upon three-pences, what anxiety might not such a denunciation produce! But such does not happen to be the present motive of publication! I write partly to shew my good-nature, and partly to shew my vanity; nor will I lay down the pen till I am satisfied one way or another.

Others have disliked the title and the motto of my paper, point out a mistake in the one, and assure me the other has been consigned to dulness by anticipation. All this may be true; *but what is that to me?* Titles and mottoes to books are like escutcheons and dignities in the hands of a king. The wise sometimes condescend

105

to *accept* of them; but none but a fool will imagine them of any real importance. We ought to depend upon intrinsic merit, and not the slender hopes of title. *Nam quæ non fecimus ipsi, vix ea nostra voco.**

For my part, I am ever ready to mistrust a promising title, and have, at some expence, been instructed not to hearken to the voice of an advertisement, let it plead never so loudly, or never so long. A countryman coming one day to Smithfield, in order to take a slice of Bartholomew-fair, found a perfect shew before every booth. The drummer, the fire-eater, the wire-walker, and the salt-box were all employed to invite him in. *Just a going; the court of the king of Prussia in all his glory; pray, gentlemen, walk in and see.* From people who generously gave so much away, the clown expected a monstrous bargain for his money when he got in. He steps up, pays his sixpence, the curtain is drawn, when too late he finds that he had the best part of the shew for nothing at the door.

A RESVERIE

Scarce a day passes in which we do not hear compliments paid to Dryden, Pope, and other writers of the last age, while not a month comes forward that is not loaded with invective against the writers of this. Strange, that our critics should be fond of giving their favours to those who are insensible of the obligation, and their dislike to these who, of all mankind, are most apt to retaliate the injury.

Even though our present writers had not equal merit with their predecessors, it would be politic to use them with ceremony. Every compliment paid them would be more agreeable, in proportion as they least deserved it. Tell a lady with an handsome face that she is pretty, she only thinks it her due; it is what she has heard a thousand times before from others, and disregards the compliment: but assure a lady, the cut of whose visage is something more plain, that she looks killing to-day, she instantly bridles up and feels the force of the well-timed flattery the whole day after. Compliments which we think are deserved, we only accept, as debts, with indifference; but those which conscience informs us we do not merit, we receive with the same gratitude that we do favours given away.

Our gentlemen, however, who preside at the distribution of literary fame, seem resolved to part with praise neither from motives of justice, or generosity; one would think, when they take pen in hand, that it was only to blot reputations, and to put their seals to the paquet which consigns every new-born effort to oblivion.

Yet, notwithstanding the republic of letters hangs at present so feebly together; though those friendships which once promoted literary fame seem now to be discontinued; though every writer who now draws the quill seems to aim at profit, as well as applause, many among them are probably laying in stores for immortality, and are provided with a sufficient stock of reputation to last the whole journey.

As I was indulging these reflections, in order to eke out the present page, I could not avoid pursuing the metaphor, of going a journey, in my imagination, and formed the following Resverie, too wild for allegory, and too regular for a dream.

I fancied myself placed in the yard of a large inn, in which there were an infinite number of waggons and stage-coaches, attended by fellows who either invited the company to take their places, or were busied in packing their baggage. Each vehicle had its inscription, shewing the place of its destination. On one I could read, *The pleasure stage-coach*; on another, *The waggon of industry*; on a third, *The vanity whim*; and on a fourth, *The landau of riches*. I had some inclination to step into each one of these, one after another; but I know not by what means I passed them by, and at last fixed my eye upon a small carriage, Berlin fashion, which seemed the most convenient vehicle at a distance in the world; and, upon my nearer approach, found it to be *The fame machine*.

107

I instantly made up to the coachman, whom I found to be an affable and seemingly good-natured fellow. He informed me, that he had but a few days ago returned from the temple of fame, to which he had been carrying Addison, Swift, Pope, Steele, Congreve, and Colley Cibber. That they made but indifferent company by the way, and that he once or twice was going to empty his berlin of the whole cargo: however, says he, I got them all safe home, with no other damage than a black eye, which Colley gave Mr Pope, and am now returned for another coachful. "If that be all, friend, said I, and if you are in want of company, I'll make one with all my heart. Open the door; I hope the machine rides easy." "Oh! for that, sir, extremely easy." But still keeping the door shut, and measuring me with his eye, "Pray, sir, have you no luggage? You seem to be a good-natured sort of a gentleman; but I don't find you have got any luggage, and I never permit any to travel with me but such as have something valuable to pay for coach-hire." Examining my pockets, I own I was not a little disconcerted at this unexpected rebuff; but considering that I carried a number of the BEE under my arm, I was resolved to open it in his eyes, and dazzle him with the splendor of the page. He read the title and contents, however, without any emotion, and assured me he had never heard of it before. "In short, friend, said he, now losing all his former respect, you must not come in. I expect better passengers; but, as you seem an harmless creature, perhaps, if there be room left, I may let you ride a while for charity."

I now took my stand by the coachman at the door, and since I could not command a seat, was resolved to be as useful as possible, and earn by my assiduity, what I could not by my merit.

The next that presented for a place, was a most whimsical figure indeed. He was hung round with papers of his own composing, not unlike those who sing ballads in the streets, and came dancing up to the door with all the confidence of instant admittance. The volubility of his motion and address prevented my being able to read more of his cargo than the word Inspector, which was written in great letters at the top of some of the papers.

He opened the coach-door himself without any ceremony, and was just slipping in, when the coachman, with as little ceremony, pulled him back. Our figure seemed perfectly angry at this repulse, and demanded gentleman's satisfaction. "Lord, sir! replied the coachman, instead of proper luggage, by your bulk you seem loaded for a West-India voyage. You are big enough, with all your papers, to crack twenty stage-coaches. Excuse me, indeed, sir, for you must not enter." Our figure now began to expostulate; he assured the coachman, that though his baggage seemed so bulky, it was perfectly light, and that he would be contented with the smallest corner of room. But Jehu was inflexible, and the carrier of the inspectors was sent to dance back again, with all his papers fluttering in the wind. We expected to have no more trouble from this quarter, when, in a few minutes, the same figure changed his appearance, like harlequin upon the stage, and with the same confidence again made his approaches, dressed in lace, and carrying nothing but a nosegay. Upon coming near, he thrust the nosegay to the coachman's nose, grasped the brass, and seemed now resolved to enter by violence. I found the struggle soon begin to grow hot, and the coachman, who was a little old, unable to continue the contest, so, in order to ingratiate myself, I stept in to his assistance, and our united efforts sent our literary Proteus, though worsted, unconquered still, clear off, dancing a rigadoon, and smelling to his own nosegay.

The person who after him appeared as candidate for a place in the stage, came up with an air not quite so confident, but somewhat however theatrical; and, instead of entering, made the coachman a very low bow, which the other returned, and desired to see his baggage; upon which he instantly produced some farces, a tragedy, and other miscellany productions. The coachman, casting his eye upon the cargoe, assured him, at present he could not possibly have a place, but hoped in time he might aspire to one, as he seemed to have read in the book of nature, without a careful perusal of which none ever found entrance at the temple of fame. "What, (replied the disappointed poet) shall my tragedy, in which I have vindicated the cause of liberty and virtue!" —————— "Follow nature, (returned the other) and never expect to find lasting fame by topics which only please from their popularity. Had you been first in the cause of freedom, or praised in virtue more than an empty name, it is possible you might have gained admittance; but at present I beg, sir, you will stand aside for another gentleman whom I see approaching."

This was a very grave personage [Johnson], whom at some distance I took for one of the most reserved, and even disagreeable figures I had seen; but as he approached, his appearance improved, and when I could distinguish him thoroughly, I perceived, that, in spite of the severity of his brow, he had one of the most good-natured countenances that could be imagined. Upon coming to open the stage door, he lifted a parcel of folios into the seat before him, but our inquisitorial coachman at once shoved them out again. "What, not take in my dictionary! exclaimed the other in a rage." "Be patient, sir, (replyed the coachman) I have drove a coach, man and boy, these two thousand years; but I do not remember to have carried above one dictionary during the whole time. That little book which I perceive peeping from one of your pockets, may I presume to ask what it contains?" "A mere trifle, (replied the author) it is called the Rambler." "The Rambler! (says the coachman) I beg, sir, you'll take your place; I have heard our ladies in the court of Apollo frequently mention it with rapture; and Clio, who happens to be a little grave, has been heard to prefer it to the Spectator; though others have observed, that the reflections, by being refined, sometimes become minute."

This grave gentleman was scarce seated, when another, whose appearance was something more modern, seemed willing to enter, yet afraid to ask. He carried in his hand a bundle of essays, of which the coachman was curious enough to inquire the contents. "These (replied the gentleman) are rhapsodies against the religion of my country." "And how can you expect to come into my coach, after thus chusing the wrong side of the question." "Ay, but I am right (replied the other;) and if you give me leave,

110

I shall in a few minutes state the argument." "Right or wrong (said the coachman) he who disturbs religion, is a blockhead, and he shall never travel in a coach of mine." "If then (said the gentleman, mustering up all his courage) if I am not to have admittance as an essayist, I hope I shall not be repulsed as an historian; the last volume of my history met with applause." "Yes, (replied the coachman) but I have heard only the first approved at the temple of fame; and as I see you have it about you, enter without further ceremony." My attention was now diverted to a crowd, who were pushing forward a person that seemed more inclined to the *stage coach of riches*; but by their means he was driven forward to the fame machine, which he, however, seemed heartily to despise. Impelled, however, by their sollicitations, he steps up, flourishing a voluminous history, and demanding admittance. "Sir, I have formerly heard your name mentioned (says the coachman) but never as an historian. Is there no other work upon which you may claim a place?" "None, replied the other, except a romance; but this is a work of too trifling a nature to claim future attention." "You mistake (says the inquisitor) a well-written romance is no such easy task as is generally imagined. I remember formerly to have carried Cervantes and Segrais, and if you think fit, you may enter." Upon our three literary travellers coming into the same coach, I listened attentively to hear what might be the conversation that passed upon this extraordinary occasion; when, instead of agreeable or entertaining dialogue, I found them grumbling at each other, and each seemed discontented with his companions. Strange! thought I to myself, that they who are thus born to enlighten the world, should still preserve the narrow prejudices of childhood, and, by disagreeing, make even the highest merit ridiculous. Were the learned and the wise to unite against the dunces of society, instead of sometimes siding into opposite parties with them, they might throw a lustre upon each other's reputation, and teach every rank of subordinate merit, if not to admire, at least not to avow dislike.

In the midst of these reflections, I perceived the coachman, unmindful of me, had now mounted the box. Several were approaching to be taken in, whose pretensions I was sensible were very just, I therefore desired him to stop, and take in more passengers; but he replied, as he had now mounted the box, it would be improper to come down; but that he should take them all, one after the other, when he should return. So he drove away, and, for myself, as I could not get in, I mounted behind, in order to hear the conversation on the way.

From: *the Citizen of the World*
or
Letters from a Chinese Philosopher Residing in London to his Friends in the East

LETTER XXVI
The character of the man in black; with some instances of his inconsistent conduct.

Tho' fond of many acquaintances, I desire an intimacy only with a few. The man in black whom I have often mentioned, is one whose friendship I cou'd wish to acquire, because he possesses my esteem. His manners it is true, are tinctured with some strange inconsistencies; and he may be justly termed an humourist in a nation of humourists. Tho' he is generous even to profusion, he affects to be thought a prodigy of parsimony and prudence; though his conversation be replete with the most sordid and selfish maxims, his heart is dilated with the most unbounded love. I have known him profess himself a man-hater, while his cheek was glowing with compassion; and while his looks were softened into pity, I have heard him use the language of the most unbounded ill nature. Some affect humanity and tenderness, others boast of having such dispositions from nature; but he is the only man I ever knew who seemed ashamed of his natural benevolence. He takes as much pains to hide his feelings as any

112

hypocrite would to conceal his indifference; but on every unguarded moment the mask drops off, and reveals him to the most superficial observer.

In one of our late excursions into the country, happening to discourse upon the provision that was made for the poor in England, he seemed amazed how any of his countrymen could be so foolishly weak as to relieve occasional objects of charity, when the laws had made such ample provision for their support. In every parish house, says he, the poor are supplied with food, cloaths, fire, and a bed to lie on; they want no more, I desire no more my self; yet still they seem discontented. I'm surprized at the inactivity of our magistrates, in not taking up such vagrants who are only a weight upon the industrious; I'm surprized that the people are found to relieve them, when they must be at the same time sensible that it, in some measure, encourages idleness, extravagance, and imposture. Were I to advise any man for whom I had the least regard, I would caution him by all means not to be imposed upon by their false pretences: let me assure you, Sir, they are impostors, every one of them; and rather merit a prison than relief.

He was proceeding in this strain earnestly, to dissuade me from an imprudence of which I am seldom guilty; when an old man who still had about him the remnants of tattered finery, implored our compassion. He assured us that he was no common beggar, but forced into the shameful profession, to support a dying wife and five hungry children. Being prepossessed against such falsehoods, his story had not the least influence upon me; but it was quite otherwise with the man in black; I could see it visibly operate upon his countenance, and effectually interrupt his harangue. I could easily perceive that his heart burned to relieve the five starving children, but he seemed ashamed to discover his weakness to me. While he thus hesitated between compassion and pride, I pretended to look another way, and he seized this opportunity of giving the poor petitioner a piece of silver, bidding him at the same time, in order that I should hear, go work for his bread, and not teize passengers with such impertinent falsehoods for the future.

As he had fancied himself quite unperceived, he continued, as we proceeded, to rail against beggars with as much animosity as before; he threw in some episodes on his own amazing prudence and œconomy, with his profound skill in discovering impostors; he explained the manner in which he would deal with beggars were he a magistrate, hinted at enlarging some of the prisons for their reception, and told two stories of ladies that were robbed by beggarmen. He was beginning a third to the same purpose, when a sailor with a wooden leg once more crossed our walks, desiring our pity, and blessing our limbs. I was for going on without taking any notice, but my friend looking wishfully upon the poor petitioner, bid me stop, and he would shew me with how much ease he could at any time detect an impostor.

He now therefore assumed a look of importance, and in an angry tone began to examine the sailor, demanding in what engagement he was thus disabled and rendered unfit for service. The sailor replied in a tone as angrily as he, that he had been an officer on board a private ship of war, and that he had lost his leg abroad in defence of those who did nothing at home. At this reply, all my friend's importance vanished in a moment; he had not a single question more to ask; he now only studied what method he should take to relieve him unobserved. He had however no easy part to act, as he was obliged to preserve the appearance of ill nature before me, and yet relieve himself by relieving the sailor. Casting therefore a furious look upon some bundles of chips which the fellow carried in a string at his back, my friend demanded how he sold his matches; but not waiting for a reply, desired, in a surly tone, to have a shilling's worth. The sailor seemed at first surprised at his demand, but soon recollecting himself, and presenting his whole bundle, Here, master, says he, take all my cargo, and a blessing into the bargain.

It is impossible to describe with what an air of triumph my friend marched off with his new purchase, he assured me that he was firmly of opinion that those fellows must have stolen their goods, who could thus afford to sell them for half value; he in-

114

formed me of several different uses to which those chips might be applied; he expatiated largely upon the savings that would result from lighting candles with a match instead of thrusting them into the fire. He averred, that he would as soon have parted with a tooth as his money to those vagabonds, unless for some valuable consideration. I cannot tell how long this panegyric upon frugality and matches might have continued, had not his attention been called off by another object more distressful than either of the former. A woman in rags, with one child in her arms, and another on her back, was attempting to sing ballads, but with such a mournful voice that it was difficult to determine whether she was singing or crying. A wretch, who, in the deepest distress still aimed at good humour, was an object my friend was by no means capable of withstanding: his vivacity, and his discourse were instantly interrupted; upon this occasion his very dissimulation had forsaken him. Even in my presence, he immediately applied his hands to his pockets, in order to relieve her; but guess his confusion, when he found he had already given away all the money he carried about him to former objects. The misery painted in the woman's visage, was not half so strongly expressed as the agony in his. He continued to search for some time, but to no purpose, till, at length, recollecting himself, with a face of ineffable good-nature, as he had no money, he put into her hands his shilling's worth of matches.

LETTER XXVII
The history of the man in black.

As there appeared something reluctantly good in the character of my companion, I must own it surprized me what could be his motives for thus concealing virtues which others take such pains to display. I was unable to repress my desire of knowing the history of a man who thus seemed to act under continual restraint, and whose benevolence was rather the effect of appetite than reason.

115

It was not however till after repeated solicitations he thought proper to gratify my curiosity. "If you are fond, says he, of hearing *hair breadth 'scapes*, my history must certainly please; for I have been for twenty years upon the very verge of starving, without ever being starved.

"My father, the younger son of a good family, was possessed of a small living in the church. His education was above his fortune, and his generosity greater than his education. Poor as he was, he had his flatterers still poorer than himself; for every dinner he gave them, they returned him an equivalent in praise; and this was all he wanted; the same ambition that actuates a monarch at the head of an army, influenced my father at the head of his table: he told the story of the ivy-tree, and that was laughed at; he repeated the jest of the two scholars and one pair of breeches, and the company laughed at that; but the story of Taffy in the sedan chair was sure to set the table in a roar, thus his pleasure encreased in proportion to the pleasure he gave; he loved all the world, and he fancied all the world loved him.

"As his fortune was but small, he lived up to the very extent of it; he had no intentions of leaving his children money, for that was dross; he was resolved they should have learning; for learning, he used to observe, was better than silver or gold. For this purpose he undertook to instruct us himself; and took as much pains to form our morals, as to improve our understanding. We were told that universal benevolence was what first cemented society; we were taught to consider all the wants of mankind as our own; to regard the *human face divine* with affection and esteem; he wound us up to be mere machines of pity, and rendered us incapable of withstanding the slightest impulse made either by real or fictitious distress; in a word, we were perfectly instructed in the art of *giving away* thousands, before we were taught the more necessary qualifications of *getting* a farthing.

"I cannot avoid imagining, that, thus refined by his lessons out of all my suspicion, and divested of even all the little cunning which nature had given me, I resembled, upon my first entrance into the busy and insidious world, one of those gladiators who

116

were exposed without armour in the amphitheatre at Rome. My father, however, who had only seen the world on one side, seemed to triumph in my superior discernment; though my whole stock of wisdom consisted in being able to talk like himself upon subjects that once were useful, because they were then topics of the busy world; but that now were utterly useless, because connected with the busy world no longer.

"The first opportunity he had of finding his expectations disappointed, was at the very middling figure I made in the university: he had flattered himself that he should soon see me rising into the foremost rank in literary reputation, but was mortified to find me utterly unnoticed and unknown. His disappointment might have been partly ascribed to his having over-rated my talents, and partly to my dislike of mathematical reasonings at a time, when my imagination and memory yet unsatisfied, were more eager after new objects, than desirous of reasoning upon those I knew. This did not, however, please my tutors, who observed, indeed, that I was a little dull; but at the same time allowed, that I seemed to be *very good natured*, and had no harm in me.

"After I had resided at college seven years, my father died, and left me – his blessing. Thus shoved from shore without ill-nature to protect, or cunning to guide, or proper stores to subsist me in so dangerous a voyage, I was obliged to embark in the wide world at twenty-two. But, in order to settle in life, my friends *advised* (for they always advise when they begin to despise us) they advised me, I say, to go into orders.

"To be obliged to wear a long wig, when I liked a short one, or a black coat, when I generally dressed in brown, I thought was such a restraint upon my liberty, that I absolutely rejected the proposal. A priest in England, is not the same mortified creature with a bonze in China; with us, not he that fasts best, but eats best, is reckoned the best liver; yet I rejected a life of luxury, indolence, and ease, from no other consideration but that boyish one of dress. So that my friends were now perfectly satisfied I was undone; and yet they thought it a pity for one who had not the least harm in him, and was so very good-natured.

117

"Poverty naturally begets dependance, and I was admitted as flatterer to a great man. At first I was surprised, that the situation of a flatterer at a great man's table could be thought disagreeable; there was no great trouble in listening attentively when his lordship spoke, and laughing when he looked round for applause. This even good-manners might have obliged me to perform. I found, however, too soon, that his lordship was a greater dunce than myself; and from that very moment my power of flattery was at an end. I now rather aimed at setting him right, than at receiving his absurdities with submission: to flatter those we do not know is an easy task; but to flatter our intimate acquaintances, all whose foibles are strongly in our eye, is drudgery insupportable. Every time I now opened my lips in praise, my falsehood went to my conscience; his lordship soon perceived me to be unfit for service; I was therefore discharged; my patron at the same time being graciously pleased to observe, that he believed I was tolerably good-natured, and had not the least harm in me.

"Disappointed in ambition I had recourse to love. A young lady, who lived with her aunt, and was possessed of a pretty fortune in her own disposal, had given me, as I fancied, some reasons to expect success. The symptoms by which I was guided were striking; she had always laughed with me at her aukward acquaintance, and at her aunt among the number; she always observed, that a man of sense would make a better husband than a fool, and I as constantly applied the observation in my own favour. She continually talked in my company of friendship and the beauties of the mind, and spoke of Mr Shrimp my rival's high-heel'd shoes with detestation. These were circumstances which I thought strongly in my favour; so after resolving, and re-resolving, I had courage enough to tell her my mind. Miss heard my proposal with serenity, seeming at the same time to study the figures of her fan. Out at last it came. There was but one small objection to complete our happiness, which was no more, than – that she was married three months before to Mr Shrimp with high-heel'd shoes! By way of consolation however she observed, that tho' I was disappointed in her, my addresses to her aunt would probably kindle her into sensibility; as the old lady always allowed me to be very good natured, and not to have the least share of harm in me.

"Yet still I had friends, numerous friends, and to them I was resolved to apply. O friendship! thou fond soother of the human breast, to thee we fly in every calamity; to thee the wretched seek for succour; on thee the care-tired son of misery fondly relies; from thy kind assistance the unfortunate always hopes relief, and may be ever sure of – disappointment! My first application was to a city scrivener, who had frequently offered to lend me money when he knew I did not want it. I informed him, that now was the time to put his friendship to the test; that I wanted to borrow a couple of hundreds for a certain occasion, and was resolved to take it up from him. And pray, Sir, cried my friend, do you want all this money? Indeed I never wanted it more, returned I. I am sorry for that, cries the scrivener, with all my heart; for they who want money when they come to borrow, will always want money when they should come to pay.

"From him I flew with indignation to one of the best friends I had in the world, and made the same request. Indeed, Mr Drybone, cries my friend, I always thought it would come to this. You know, sir, I would not advise you but for your own good; but your conduct has hitherto been ridiculous in the highest degree, and some of your acquaintance always thought you a very silly fellow; let me see, you want two hundred pounds; do you want only two hundred, sir, exactly? To confess a truth, returned I, I shall want three hundred; but then I have another friend from whom I can borrow the rest. Why then, replied my friend, if you would take my advice; and you know I should not presume to advise you but for your own good, I would recommend it to you to borrow the whole sum from that other friend; and then one note will serve for all, you know.

"Poverty now began to come fast upon me, yet instead of growing more provident or cautious as I grew poor, I became every day more indolent and simple. A friend was arrested for fifty pounds, I was unable to extricate him except by becoming his bail. When at liberty he fled from his creditors, and left me to take his place. In prison I expected greater satisfactions than I had enjoyed at large. I hoped to converse with men in this new world simple and believing like myself, but I found them as cunning and as cautious as those in the world I had left behind. They spunged up my money whilst it lasted, borrowed my coals and never paid them, and cheated me when I played at cribbage. All this was done because they believed me to be very good-natured, and knew that I had no harm in me.

"Upon my first entrance into this mansion, which is to some the abode of despair, I felt no sensations different from those I experienced abroad. I was now on one side the door, and those who were unconfined were on the other; this was all the difference between us. At first indeed I felt some uneasiness, in considering how I should be able to provide this week for the wants of the week ensuing; but after some time, if I found myself sure of eating one day, I never troubled my head how I was to be supplied another. I seized every precarious meal with the utmost good humour, indulged no rants of spleen at my situation, never called down heaven and all the stars to behold me dining upon an halfpenny-worth of radishes; my very companions were taught to believe that I liked sallad better than mutton. I contented myself with thinking, that all my life I should either eat white bread or brown; considered that all that happened was best, laughed when I was not in pain, took the world as it went, and read Tacitus often, for want of more books and company.

"How long I might have continued in this torpid state of simplicity I cannot tell, had I not been rouzed by seeing an old acquaintance, whom I knew to be a prudent blockhead preferred to a place in the government. I now found that I had pursued a wrong track, and that the true way of being able to relieve others, was first to aim at independance myself. My immediate care, therefore, was to leave my present habitation, and make an entire reformation in my conduct and behaviour. For a free, open, undesigning deportment, I put on that of closeness, prudence and œconomy. One of the most heroic actions I ever performed, and for which I shall praise myself as long as I live, was the refusing half a crown to an old acquaintance, at the time when he wanted it, and I had it to spare; for this alone I deserve to be decreed an ovation.

"I now therefore pursued a course of uninterrupted frugality, seldom wanted a dinner, and was consequently invited to twenty. I soon began to get the character of a saving hunks that had money; and insensibly grew into esteem. Neighbours have asked my advice in the disposal of their daughters, and I have always taken care not to give any. I have contracted a friendship with an alderman, only by observing, that if we take a farthing from a thousand pound it will be a thousand pound no longer. I have been invited to a pawnbroker's table, by pretending to hate gravy; and am now actually upon treaty of marriage with a rich widow, for only having observed that the bread was rising. If ever I am asked a question, whether I know it or not, instead of answering, I only smile and look wise. If a charity is proposed, I go about with the hat, but put nothing in myself. If a wretch solicits my pity, I observe that the world is filled with impostors, and take a certain method of not being deceived by never relieving. In short, I now find the truest way of finding esteem even from the indigent, is *to give away nothing, and thus have much in our power to give.*"

LETTER XC
The English subject to the spleen.

When the men of this country are once turned of thirty, they regularly retire every year at proper intervals to lie in of the *spleen*. The vulgar, unfurnished with the luxurious comforts of the soft cussion, down bed, and easy-chair, are obliged when the fit is on them, to nurse it up by drinking, idleness and ill-humour. In such dispositions, unhappy is the foreigner who happens to cross them; his long chin, tarnished coat, or pinched hat, are sure to

121

receive no quarter. If they meet no foreigner however to fight with, they are in such cases generally content with beating each other.

The rich, as they have more sensibility, are operated upon with greater violence by this disorder. Different from the poor, instead of becoming more insolent, they grow totally unfit for opposition. A general here, who would have faced a culverin when well, if the fit be on him, shall hardly find courage to snuff a candle. An admiral, who could have opposed a broadside without shrinking, shall sit whole days in his chamber, mobbed up in double night-caps, shuddering at the intrusive breeze, and distinguishable from his wife only by his black beard and heavy eyebrows.

In the country this disorder mostly attacks the fair sex, in town it is most unfavourable to the men. A lady, who has pined whole years amidst cooing doves and complaining nightingales, in rural retirement, shall resume all her vivacity in one night at a city gaming-table; her husband who roar'd, hunted, and got drunk at home, shall grow splenetic in town in proportion to his wife's good humour. Upon their arrival in London, they exchange their disorders. In consequence of her parties and excursions, he puts on the furred cap and scarlet stomacher, and perfectly resembles an Indian husband, who when his wife is safely delivered, permits her to transact business abroad, while he undergoes all the formality of keeping his bed, and receiving all the condolence in her place.

But those who reside constantly in town, owe this disorder mostly to the influence of the weather. It is impossible to describe what a variety of transmutations an east wind shall produce; it has been known to change a Lady of fashion into a parlour couch; an Alderman into a plate of custards, and a dispenser of justice into a rat trap. Even Philosophers themselves are not exempt from its influence; it has often converted a Poet into a coral and bells, and a patriot Senator into a dumb waiter.

Some days ago I went to visit the man in black, and entered his house with that chearfulness, which the certainty of a favourable reception always inspires. Upon opening the door of his apartment, I found him with the most rueful face imaginable in a morning gown and flannel night-cap, earnestly employed in learning to blow the German flute. Struck with the absurdity of a man in the decline of life, thus blowing away all his constitution and spirits, even without the consolation of being musical; I ventured to ask what could induce him to attempt learning so difficult an instrument so late in life. To this he made no reply, but groaning, and still holding the flute to his lip, continued to gaze at me for some moments very angrily, and then proceeded to practise his gammut as before. After having produced a variety of the most hideous notes in nature; at last turning to me, he demanded, whether I did not think he had made a surprizing progress in two days? You see, continues he, I have got the Ambusheer already, and as for fingering, my master tells me, I shall have that in a few lessons more. I was so much astonished with this instance of inverted ambition, that I knew not what to reply, but soon discerned the cause of all his absurdities; my friend was under a metamorphosis by the power of spleen, and flute-blowing was unluckily become his adventitious passion.

In order therefore to banish his anxiety imperceptibly, by seeming to indulge it, I began to descant on those gloomy topics by which Philosophers often get rid of their own spleen, by communicating it; the wretchedness of a man in this life, the happiness of some wrought out of the miseries of others, the necessity that wretches should expire under punishment, that rogues might enjoy affluence in tranquility; I led him on from the inhumanity of the rich to the ingratitude of the beggar; from the insincerity of refinement to the fierceness of rusticity; and at last had the good fortune to restore him to his usual serenity of temper, by permitting him to expatiate upon all the modes of human misery.

"Some nights ago, says my friend, sitting alone by my fire, I happened to look into an account of the detection of a set of men called the thief-takers. I read over the many hideous cruelties of those haters of mankind, of their pretended friendship to wretches they meant to betray, of their sending men out to rob and then hanging them. I could not avoid sometimes interrupting the narrative by crying out, *Yet these are men!* As I went on, I was informed that they had lived by this practice several years, and had been enriched by the price of blood, *and yet*, cried I, *I have been sent into this world, and am desired to call these men my brothers!* I read that the very man who led the condemned wretch to the gallows, was he who falsely swore his life away; *and yet*, continued I *that perjurer had just such a nose, such lips, such hands and such eyes as Newton*. I at last came to the account of the wretch that was searched after robbing one of the thief-takers of half a crown. Those of the confederacy knew that he had got but that single half crown in the world; after a long search therefore, which they knew would be fruitless, and taking from him the half crown, which they knew was all he had, one of the gang compassionately cried out, *Alas, poor creature let him keep all the rest he has got, it will do him service in Newgate, where we are sending him*. This was an instance of such complicated guilt and hypocrisy, that I threw down the book in an agony of rage, and began to think with malice of all the human kind. I sat silent for some minutes, and soon perceiving the ticking of my watch beginning to grow noisy and troublesome, I quickly placed it out of hearing, and strove to resume my serenity. But the watch-man soon gave me a second alarm. I had scarcely recovered from this, when my peace was assaulted by the wind at my window; and when that ceased to blow, I listened for death-watches in the wainscot. I now found my whole system discomposed, I strove to find a resource in philosophy and reason; but what could I oppose, or where direct my blow, when I could see no enemy to combat. I saw no misery approaching, nor knew any I had to fear, yet still I was miserable. Morning came, I sought for tranquility in dissipation, sauntered from one place of public resort to another, but found myself disagreeable to my acquaintance, and ridiculous to others. I tried at different times dancing, fencing, and riding, I solved geometrical problems, shaped tobacco-stoppers, wrote verses and cut paper. At last I placed my affections on music, and find, that earnest employment if it cannot cure, at least will palliate every anxiety." Adieu.

The fondness of some, to admire the writing of lords, &c.

It is surprizing what an influence titles shall have upon the mind, even though these titles be of our own making. Like children we dress up the puppets in finery, and then stand in astonishment at the plastic wonder. I have been told of a rat-catcher here, who strolled for a long time about the villages near town, without finding any employment; at last, however, he thought proper to take the title of his Majesty's Rat-catcher in ordinary, and this succeeded beyond his expectations; when it was known that he caught rats at court, all were ready to give him countenance and employment.

But of all the people, they who make books seem most perfectly sensible of the advantage of titular dignity. All seem convinced, that a book written by vulgar hands, can neither instruct nor improve; none but Kings, Chams, and Mandarines, can write with any probability of success. If the titles inform me right, not only Kings and Courtiers, but Emperors themselves in this country, periodically supply the press.

A man here who should write, and honestly confess that he wrote for bread, might as well send his manuscript to fire the baker's oven; not one creature will read him; all must be court-bred poets, or pretend at least to be court-bred, who can expect to please. Should the caitiff fairly avow a design of emptying our pockets and filling his own, every reader would instantly forsake him; even those, who write for bread themselves, would combine to worry him, perfectly sensible, that his attempts only served to take the bread out of their mouths.

And yet this silly prepossession the more amazes me, when I consider, that almost all the excellent productions in wit that have appeared here, were purely the offspring of necessity; their Drydens, Butlers, Otways, and Farquhars, were all writers for bread. Believe me, my friend, hunger has a most amazing faculty of sharpening the genius; and he who with a full belly, can think like a hero, after a course of fasting, shall rise to the sublimity

125

of a demi-god.

But what will most amaze, is, that this very set of men, who are now so much depreciated by fools, are however the very best writers they have among them at present. For my own part, were I to buy a hat, I would not have it from a stocking-maker, but an hatter; were I to buy shoes, I should not go to the taylor's for that purpose. It is just so with regard to wit: did I, for my life, desire to be well served, I would apply only to those who made it their trade, and lived by it. You smile at the oddity of my opinion; but be assured, my friend, that wit is in some measure mechanical; and that a man long habituated to catch at even its resemblance, will at last be happy enough to possess the sub-stance: by a long habit of writing he acquires a justness of think-ing, and a mastery of manner, which holiday-writers, even with ten times his genius, may vainly attempt to equal.

How then are they deceived, who expect from title, dignity, and exterior circumstance, an excellence, which is in some measure acquired by habit, and sharpened by necessity; you have seen, like me, many literary reputations promoted by the influence of fashion, which have scarce survived the possessor; you have seen the poor hardly earn the little reputation they acquired, and their merit only acknowledged when they were incapable of enjoying the pleasures of popularity; such, however, is the reputation worth possessing, that which is hardly earned is hardly lost. Adieu.

LETTER XCVII

Almost every subject of literature, has been already exhausted.

It is usual for the booksellers here, when a book has given univ-ersal pleasure upon one subject, to bring out several more upon the same plan; which are sure to have purchasers and readers from that desire which all men have to view a pleasing object on every side. The first performance serves rather to awake than

126

satisfy attention; and when that is once moved, the slightest effort serves to continue its progression; the merit of the first diffuses a light sufficient to illuminate the succeeding efforts; and no other subject can be relished, till that is exhausted. A stupid work coming thus immediately in the train of an applauded performance, weans the mind from the object of its pleasure; and resembles the sponge thrust into the mouth of a discharged culverin, in order to adapt it for a new explosion.

This manner, however, of drawing off a subject, or a peculiar mode of writing to the dregs, effectively precludes a revival of that subject or manner for some time for the future; the sated reader turns from it with a kind of literary nausea; and though the titles of books are the part of them most read, yet he has scarce perseverance enough to wade through the title page.

Of this number I own myself one; I am now grown callous to several subjects, and different kinds of composition: whether such originally pleased I will not take upon me to determine; but at present I spurn a new book merely upon seeing its name in an advertisement; nor have the smallest curiosity to look beyond the first leaf, even though in the second the author promises his own face neatly engraved on copper.

I am become a perfect Epicure in reading; plain beef or solid mutton will never do. I am for a Chinese dish of bear's claws and bird's nests. I am for sauce strong with assafœtida, or fuming with garlic. For this reason there are an hundred very wise, learned, virtuous, well-intended productions that have no charms for me. Thus, for the soul of me, I could never find courage nor grace enough to wade above two pages deep into *Thoughts upon God and Nature*, or *Thoughts upon Providence*, or *Thoughts upon Free Grace*, or indeed into Thoughts upon any thing at all. I can no longer meditate with Meditations for every day in the year; Essays upon divers subjects cannot allure me, though never so interesting; and as for Funeral Sermons, or even Thanksgiving Sermons, I can neither weep with the one, nor rejoice with the other.

But it is chiefly in gentle poetry, where I seldom look farther

127

than the title. The truth is, I take up books to be told something new; but here, as it is now managed, the reader is told nothing. He opens the book, and there finds very good words, truly, and much exactness of rhyme, but no information. A parcel of gaudy images pass on before his imagination like the figures in a dream; but curiosity, induction, reason, and the whole train of affections are fast asleep. The *jocunda et idonea vitæ*; those sallies which mend the heart while they amuse the fancy, are quite forgotten: so that a reader who would take up some modern applauded performances of this kind, must, in order to be pleased, first leave his good sense behind him, take for his recompence and guide bloated and compound epithet, and dwell on paintings, just indeed, because laboured with minute exactness.

If we examine, however, our internal sensations, we shall find ourselves but little pleased with such laboured vanities; we shall find that our applause rather proceeds from a kind of contagion caught up from others, and which we contribute to diffuse, than from what we privately feel. There are some subjects of which almost all the world perceive the futility; yet all combine in imposing upon each other, as worthy of praise. But chiefly this imposition obtains in literature, where men publicly contemn what they relish with rapture in private, and approve abroad what has given them disgust at home. The truth is, we deliver those criticisms in public which are supposed to be best calculated not to do justice to the author, but to impress others with an opinion of our superior discernment.

But let works of this kind, which have already come off with such applause, enjoy it all. It is neither my wish to diminish, as I was never considerable enough to add to their fame. But for the future I fear there are many poems, of which I shall find spirits to read but the title. In the first place, all odes upon winter, or summer, or autumn; in short all odes, epodes, and monodies whatsoever, shall hereafter be deemed too polite, classical, obscure, and refined, to be read, and entirely above human comprehension. Pastorals are pretty enough – for those that like them – but to me Thyrsis is one of the most insipid fellows I ever conversed with; and as for Corridon, I do not chuse his company. Elegies and epistles are very fine to those to whom they are addressed; and as for epic poems, I am generally able to discover the whole plan in reading the two first pages.

Tragedies, however, as they are now made, are good instructive moral *sermons* enough; and it would be a fault not to be pleased with *good things*. There I learn several great truths; as, that it is impossible to see into the ways of futurity; that punishment always attends the villain, that love is the fond soother of the human breast, that we should not resist heaven's will, for in resisting heaven's will, heaven's will is resisted; with several other sentiments equally new, delicate and striking. Every new tragedy therefore I shall go to see; for reflections of this nature make a tolerable harmony, when mixed up with a proper quantity of drum, trumpet, thunder, lightening, or the scene shifter's whistle. Adieu.

LETTER CXIX
On the distresses of the poor, exemplified in the life of a private centinel.

The misfortunes of the great, my friend, are held up to engage our attention, are enlarged upon in tones of declamation, and the world is called upon to gaze at the noble sufferers; they have at once the comfort of admiration and pity.

Yet where is the magnanimity of bearing misfortunes when the whole world is looking on? Men in such circumstances can act bravely even from motives of vanity. He only who, in the vale of obscurity, can brave adversity, who without friends to encourage, acquaintances to pity, or even without hope to alleviate his distresses, can behave with tranquility and indifference, is truly great: whether peasant or courtier, he deserves admiration, and should be held up for our imitation and respect.

The miseries of the poor are however entirely disregarded; tho' some undergo more real hardships in one day, than the great in

129

their whole lives. It is indeed inconceivable what difficulties the meanest English sailor or soldier endures without murmuring or regret. Every day is to him a day of misery, and yet he bears his hard fate without repining.

With what indignation do I hear the heroes of tragedy complain of misfortunes and hardships, whose greatest calamity is founded in arrogance and pride. Their severest distresses are pleasures, compared to what many of the adventuring poor every day sustain, without murmuring. These may eat, drink, and sleep, have slaves to attend them, and are sure of subsistence for life, while many of their fellow-creatures are obliged to wander, without a friend to comfort or to assist them, find enmity in every law, and are too poor to obtain even justice.

I have been led into these reflections from accidentally meeting some days ago a poor fellow begging at one of the outlets of this town, with a wooden leg. I was curious to learn what had reduced him to his present situation; and after giving him what I thought proper, desired to know the history of his life and misfortunes, and the manner in which he was reduced to his present distress. The disabled soldier, for such he was, with an intrepidity truly British, leaning on his crutch, put himself into an attitude to comply with my request, and gave me his history as follows:

"As for misfortunes, Sir, I can't pretend to have gone through more than others. Except the loss of my limb, and my being obliged to beg, I don't know any reason, thank heaven, that I have to complain: there are some who have lost both legs, and an eye; but, thank heaven, it is not quite so bad with me.

"My father was a labourer in the country, and died when I was five years old; so I was put upon the parish. As he had been a wandering sort of a man, the parishioners were not able to tell to what parish I belonged, or where I was born; so they sent me to another parish, and that parish sent me to a third; till at last it was thought I belonged to no parish at all. At length, however, they fixed me. I had some disposition to be a scholar, and had actually learned my letters; but the master of the workhouse put me to business as soon as I was able to handle a mallet.

"Here I lived an easy kind of life for five years. I only wrought ten hours in the day, and had my meat and drink provided for my labour. It is true, I was not suffered to stir far from the house, for fear I should run away: but what of that, I had the liberty of the whole house, and the yard before the door, and that was enough for me.

"I was next bound out to a farmer, where I was up both early and late, but I ate and drank well, and liked my business well enough, till he died. Being then obliged to provide for myself, I was resolved to go and seek my fortune. Thus I lived, and went from town to town, working when I could get employment, and starving when I could get none, and might have lived so still: But happening one day to go through a field belonging to a magistrate, I spy'd a hare crossing the path just before me. I believe the devil put it in my head to fling my stick at it: well, what will you have on't? I killed the hare, and was bringing it away in triumph, when the justice himself met me: he called me a villain, and collaring me, desired I would give an account of myself. I began immediately to give a full account of all that I knew of my breed, seed, and generation: but though I gave a very long account, the justice said, I could give no account of myself; so I was indicted, and found guilty of being poor, and sent to Newgate, in order to be transported to the plantations.

"People may say this and that of being in jail; but for my part, I found Newgate as agreeable a place as ever I was in, in all my life. I had my belly full to eat and drink, and did no work; but alas, this kind of life was too good to last for ever! I was taken out of prison, after five months, put on board of a ship, and sent off with two hundred more. Our passage was but indifferent, for we were all confined in the hold, and died very fast, for want of sweet air and provisions; but for my part, I did not want meat, because I had a fever all the way: providence was kind, when provisions grew short, it took away my desire of eating. When we came ashore, we were sold to the planters. I was bound for seven years, and as I was no scholar, for I had forgot my letters, I was obliged to work among the negroes; and served out my

131

time, as in duty bound to do.

"When my time was expired, I worked my passage home, and glad I was to see Old England again, because I loved my country. O liberty, liberty, liberty! that is the property of every Englishman, and I will die in its defence: I was afraid, however, that I should be indicted for a vagabond once more, so did not much care to go into the country, but kept about town, and did little jobs when I could get them. I was very happy in this manner for some time; till one evening, coming home from work, two men knocked me down, and then desired me to stand still. They belonged to a press-gang; I was carried before the justice, and as I could give no account of my self, (that was the thing that always hobbled me,) I had my choice left, whether to go on board a man of war, or list for a soldier. I chose to be a soldier; and in this post of a gentleman I served two campaigns, was at the battles in Flanders, and received but one wound through the breast, which is troublesome to this day.

"When the peace came on, I was discharged; and as I could not work, because my wound was sometimes painful, I listed for a landman in the East India company's service. I here fought the French in six pitched battles; and verily believe, that if I could read or write, our captain would have given me promotion, and made me a corporal. But that was not my good fortune, I soon fell sick, and when I became good for nothing, got leave to return home again with forty pounds in my pocket, which I saved in the service. This was at the beginning of the present war, so I hoped to be set on shore, and to have the pleasure of spending my money; but the government wanted men, and I was pressed again, before ever I could set foot on shore.

"The boatswain found me, as he said, an obstinate fellow: he swore that I understood my business perfectly well, but that I pretended sickness merely to be idle: God knows, I knew nothing of sea-business: He beat me without considering what he was about. But still my forty pounds was some comfort to me under every beating; the money was my comfort, and the money I might have had to this day; but that our ship was taken by the French, and so I lost it all!

132

"Our crew was carried into a French prison, and many of them died, because they were not used to live in a jail; but for my part it was nothing to me, for I was seasoned. One night however, as I was sleeping on the bed of boards, with a warm blanket about me, (for I always loved to lie well,) I was awaked by the boatswain, who had a dark lanthorn in his hand. 'Jack, says he to me, will you knock out the French centry's brains?' 'I don't care, says I, striving to keep myself awake, if I lend a hand.' 'Then follow me, says he, and I hope we shall do business.' So up I got, and tied my blanket, which was all the cloaths I had, about my middle, and went with him to fight the Frenchmen: we had no arms; but one Englishman is able to beat five French at any time; so we went down to the door, where both the centries were posted, and rushing upon them, seized their arms in a moment, and knocked them down. From thence, nine of us ran together to the key, and seizing the first boat we met, got out of the harbour, and put to sea: we had not been here three days before we were taken up by an English privateer, who was glad of so many good hands; and we consented to run our chance. However, we had not so much luck as we expected. In three days we fell in with a French man of war, of forty guns, while we had but twenty three; so to it we went. The fight lasted for three hours, and I verily believe we should have taken the Frenchman, but unfortunately, we lost almost all our men, just as we were going to get the victory. I was once more in the power of the French, and I believe it would have gone hard with me, had I been brought back to my old jail in Brest: but by good fortune, we were re-taken, and carried to England once more.

"I had almost forgot to tell you, that in this last engagement I was wounded in two places; I lost four fingers of the left hand, and my leg was shot off. Had I the good fortune to have lost my leg and use of my hand on board a king's ship, and not a privateer, I should have been entitled to cloathing and maintenance during the rest of my life, but that was not my chance; one man is born with a silver spoon in his mouth, and another with a wooden ladle. However, blessed be God, I enjoy good health, and have no enemy in this world that I know of, but the French, and the Justice of Peace."

Thus saying, he limped off, leaving my friend and me in admiration of his intrepidity and content; nor could we avoid acknowledging, that an habitual acquaintance with misery, is the truest school of fortitude and philosophy. Adieu.

The revolution in low life

To the Editor of Lloyd's Evening Post

Sir,

I spent part of the last summer in a little village, distant about fifty miles from town, consisting of near an hundred houses. It lay entirely out of the road of commerce, and was inhabited by a race of men who followed the primeval profession of agriculture for several generations. Though strangers to opulence, they were unacquainted with distress; few of them were known either to acquire a fortune or to die in indigence. By a long intercourse and frequent intermarriages they were all become in a manner one family; and, when the work of the day was done, spent the night agreeably in visits at each other's houses. Upon these occasions the poor traveller and stranger were always welcome; and they kept up the stated days of festivity with the strictest observance. They were merry at Christmas and mournful in Lent, got drunk on St George's-day, and religiously cracked nuts on Michaelmas-eve.

Upon my first arrival I felt a secret pleasure in observing this happy community. The chearfulness of the old, and the blooming beauty of the young, was no disagreeable change to one like me, whose whole life had been spent in cities. But my satisfaction was soon repressed, when I understood that they were shortly to leave this abode of felicity, of which they and their ancestors had been in possession time immemorial, and that they had received orders to seek for a new habitation. I was informed that a Merchant of immense fortune in London, who had lately purchased the estate on which they lived, intended to lay the whole out in a seat of pleasure for himself. I staid 'till the day on which they were compelled to remove, and own I never felt so sincere a concern before.

I was grieved to see a generous, virtuous race of men, who should be considered as the strength and ornament of their country, torn from their little habitations, and driven out to meet poverty and hardship among strangers. No longer to earn and enjoy the fruits of their labour, they were now going to toil as hirelings under some rigid Master, to flatter the opulent for a precarious meal, and to leave their children the inheritance of want and slavery. The modest matron followed her husband in tears, and often looked back at the little mansion where she had passed her life in innocence, and to which she was never more to return; while the beautiful daughter parted for ever from her Lover, who was now become too poor to maintain her as his wife. All the connexions of kindred were now irreparably broken; their neat gardens and well cultivated fields were left to desolation.

*Strata jacent passim, hominumque boumque labores.**

Such was their misery, and I could wish that this were the only instance of such migrations of late. But I am informed that nothing is at present more common than such revolutions. In almost every part of the kingdom the laborious husbandman has been reduced, and the lands are now either occupied by some general undertaker, or turned into enclosures destined for the purposes of amusement or luxury. Wherever the traveller turns, while he sees one part of the inhabitants of the country becoming immensely rich, he sees the other growing miserably poor, and the happy equality of condition now entirely removed.

Let others felicitate their country upon the encrease of foreign commerce and the extension of our foreign conquests; but for my

135

part, this new introduction of wealth gives me but very little satisfaction. Foreign commerce, as it can be managed only by a few, tends proportionably to enrich only a few; neither moderate fortunes nor moderate abilities can carry it on; thus it tends rather to the accumulation of immense wealth in the hands of some, than to a diffusion of it among all; it is calculated rather to make individuals rich, than to make the aggregate happy.

Wherever we turn we shall find those governments that have pursued foreign commerce with too much assiduity at length becoming Aristocratical; and the immense property, thus necessarily acquired by some, has swallowed up the liberties of all. Venice, Genoa, and Holland, are little better at present than retreats for tyrants and prisons for slaves. The Great, indeed, boast of their liberties there, and they have liberty. The poor boast of liberty too; but, alas, they groan under the most rigorous oppression.

A country, thus parcelled out among the rich alone, is of all others the most miserable. The Great, in themselves, perhaps, are not so bad as they are generally represented; but I have almost ever found the dependents and favourites of the Great, strangers to every sentiment of honour and generosity. Wretches, who, by giving up their own dignity to those above them, insolently exact the same tribute from those below. A country, therefore, where the inhabitants are thus divided into the very rich and very poor, is, indeed, of all others the most helpless; without courage and without strength; neither enjoying peace within itself, and, after a time, unable to resist foreign invasion.

I shall conclude this paper with a picture of Italy just before its conquest, by Theodoric the Ostrogoth. "The whole country was at that time (says the Historian) one garden of pleasure; the seats of the great men of Rome covered the face of the whole kingdom; and even their villas were supplied with provisions not of their own growth, but produced in distant countries, where they were more industrious. But in proportion as Italy was then beautiful, and its possessors rich, it was also weak and defenceless. The rough peasant and hardy husbandman had been long obliged to seek for liberty and subsistence in Britain or Gaul; and, by leaving their native country, brought with them all the strength of the nation. There was none now to resist an invading army, but the slaves of the nobility or the effeminate citizens of Rome, the one without motive, the other without strength to make any opposition. They were easily, therefore, overcome, by a people more savage indeed, but far more brave than they."

From *An History of the Earth and Animated Nature*

THE POOR MAN'S COW

There are many of our peasantry that have no other possession but a cow; and even of the advantages resulting from this most useful creature, the poor are but the nominal possessors. Its flesh they cannot pretend to taste, since then their whole riches are at once destroyed; its calf they are obliged to fatten for sale, since veal is a delicacy they could not make any pretensions to; its very milk is wrought into butter and cheese for the tables of their masters; while they have no share even in their own possession, but the choice of their market. I cannot bear to hear the rich crying out for liberty, while they thus starve their fellow creatures, and feed them up with an imaginary good, while they monopolize the real benefits of nature.... A piece of beef hung up [in Germany, Poland, and Switzerland] is considered an elegant piece of furniture, which, though seldom touched, at least it argues the possessor's opulence and ease. But it is very different, for some years past, in this country, where our lower rustics at least are utterly unable to purchase meat any part of the year, and by them even butter is considered as an article of extravagance.

THE PARTRIDGE

In England, where the partridge is much scarcer [than in France], and a great deal dearer, it is still a favourite delicacy at the tables of the rich; and the desire of keeping it to themselves, has induced them to make laws for its preservation, no way harmonizing with the general spirit of English legislation. What can be more arbitrary than to talk of preserving the game; which, when defined, means no more than that the poor shall abstain from what the rich have taken a fancy to keep for themselves? If these birds could, like a cock or a hen, be made legal property, could they be taught to keep within certain districts, and only feed on those grounds that belong to the man whose entertainments they improve, it then might, with some shew of justice, be admitted, that as a man fed them so he might claim them. But this is not the case; nor is it in any man's power to lay a restraint upon the liberty of these birds, that, when let loose, put no limits to their excursions. They feed every where; upon every man's ground; and no man can say, these birds are fed only by me. Those birds which are nourished by all, belong to all; nor can any one man, or any set of men, lay claim to them, when still continuing in a state of nature.

I never walked out about the environs of Paris, that I did not consider the immense quantity of game that was running almost tame on every side of me, as a badge of the slavery of the people; and what they wished me to observe as an object of triumph, I always regarded with a kind of secret compassion: yet this people have no game-laws for the remoter parts of the kingdom; the game is only preserved in a few places for the king; and is free in most places else. In England, the prohibition is general; and the peasant has not a right to what even slaves, as he is taught to call them, are found to possess.

Addison, in some beautiful Latin lines, inserted in the *Spectator*, is entirely of opinion that birds observe a strict chastity of manners, and never admit the caresses of a different tribe.

> Chaste are their instincts, faithful is their fire,
> No foreign beauty tempts to false desire:
> The snow-white vesture, and the glittering crown,
> The simple plumage, or the glossy down,
> Prompt not their love. The patriot bird pursues
> His well acquainted tints, and kindred hues.
> Hence through their tribes no mix'd polluted flame,
> No monster breed to mark the groves with shame:
> But the chaste blackbird, to its partner true,
> Thinks black alone is beauty's favourite hue:
> The nightingale, with mutual passion blest,
> Sings to its mate, and nightly charms the nest:
> While the dark owl, to court his partner flies,
> And owns his offspring in their yellow eyes.

But whatever may be the poet's opinion, the probability is against this fidelity among the smaller tenants of the grove. The great birds are much more true to their species than these; and, of consequence, the varieties among them are more few.... But it is otherwise with the small birds we are describing; it requires very little trouble to make a species between a goldfinch and a canary-bird, between a linnet and a lark.

THE ROOK

The rook, as is well known, builds in woods and forests in the neighbourhood of man, and sometimes makes choice of groves in the very midst of cities for the place of its retreat and security. In these it establishes a kind of legal constitution, by which all intruders are excluded from coming to live among them, and none suffered to build but acknowledged natives of the place. I have often amused myself with observing their plan of policy from my window in the Temple, that looks upon a grove where they have made a colony in the midst of the city. At the commencement of spring, the rookery, which during the continuance of winter seemed to have been deserted, or only guarded by about five or six, like old soldiers in a garrison, now begins to be once more frequented; and in a short time all the bustle and hurry of business is fairly commenced. Where these numbers resided during the winter is not easy to guess; perhaps in the trees of hedge-rows to be nearer their food. In spring, however, they cultivate their native trees; and, in the places where they were themselves hatched, they prepare to propagate a future progeny.

They keep together in pairs; and when the offices of courtship are over, they prepare for making their nests and laying. The old inhabitants of the place are all already provided; the nest which served them for years before, with a little trimming and dressing will serve very well again; the difficulty of nestling lies only upon the young ones who have no nest, and must therefore get up one as well as they can. But not only the materials are wanting, but also the place in which to fix it. Every part of a tree will not do for this purpose, as some branches may not be sufficiently forked; others may not be sufficiently strong; and still others may be too much exposed to the rockings of the wind. The male and female upon this occasion are, for some days, seen examining all the trees of the grove very attentively; and when they have fixed upon a branch that seems fit for their purpose, they continue to sit upon and observe it very sedulously for two or three days longer. The place being thus determined upon, they begin to gather the materials for their nest; such as sticks and fibrous roots, which they regularly dispose in the most substantial manner. But here a new and unexpected obstacle arises. It often happens that the young couple have made choice of a place too near the mansion of an older pair, who do not chuse to be incommoded by such troublesome neighbours. A quarrel therefore instantly

140

ensues; in which the old ones are always victorious.

The young couple, thus expelled, are obliged again to go through the fatigues of deliberating, examining, and chusing; and having taken care to keep their due distance, the nest begins again, and their industry deserves commendation. But their alacrity is often too great in the beginning; they soon grow weary of bringing the materials of their nest from distant places; and they very easily perceive that sticks may be provided nearer home, with less honesty indeed, but some degree of address. Away they go, therefore, to pilfer as fast as they can; and wherever they see a nest unguarded, they take care to rob it of the very choicest sticks of which it is composed. But these thefts never go unpunished; and probably upon complaint being made there is a general punishment inflicted. I have seen eight or ten rooks come upon such occasions, and setting upon the new nest of the young couple all at once, tear it to pieces in a moment.

At length, therefore, the young pair find the necessity of going more regularly and honestly to work. While one flies to fetch the materials, the other sits upon the tree to guard it; and thus in the space of three or four days, with a skirmish now and then between, the pair have fitted up a commodious nest composed of sticks without, and of fibrous roots and long grass within. From the instant the female begins to lay, all hostilities are at an end; not one of the whole grove, that a little before treated her so rudely, will now venture to molest her; so that she brings forth her brood with patient tranquility. Such is the severity with which even native rooks are treated by each other; but if a foreign rook should attempt to make himself a denizen of their society, he would meet with no favour; the whole grove would at once be up in arms against him, and expel him without mercy.

Those who have walked in an evening by the sedgy sides of unfrequented rivers, must remember a variety of notes from different water-fowl: the loud scream of the wild goose, the croaking of the mallard, the whining of the lapwing, and the tremulous neighing of the jack-snipe. But of all those sounds, there is none so dismally hollow as the booming of the bittern. It is impossible for words to give those who have not heard this evening-call an adequate idea of its solemnity. It is like the interrupted bellowing of a bull, but hollower and louder, and is heard at a mile's distance, as if issuing from some formidable being that resided at the bottom of the waters.

The bird, however, that produces this terrifying sound is not so big as an heron, with a weaker bill, and not above four inches long. It differs from the heron chiefly in its colour, which is in general of a paleish yellow, spotted and barred with black. Its wind-pipe is fitted to produce the sound for which it is remarkable; the lower part of it dividing into the lungs is supplied with a thin loose membrane, that can be filled with a large body of air and exploded at pleasure. These bellowing explosions are chiefly heard from the beginning of spring to the end of autumn; and, however awful they may seem to us, are the calls to courtship, or of connubial felicity.

I remember in the place where I was a boy with what terror this bird's note affected the whole village; they considered it as the presage of some sad event; and generally found or made one to succeed it. I do not speak ludicrously; but if any person in the neighbourhood died, they supposed it could not be otherwise, for the night-raven had foretold it; but if nobody happened to die, the death of a cow or a sheep gave completion to the prophecy.

The place these birds chiefly chuse to breed in, is in some island surrounded with sedgy moors, where men seldom resort; and in such situations I have often seen the ground so strewed with eggs and nests, that one could scarce take a step, without treading upon some of them. As soon as a stranger intrudes upon these retreats, the whole colony is up, and an hundred different screams are heard from every quarter. The arts of the lapwing to allure men or dogs from her nest, are perfectly amusing. When she perceives the enemy approaching, she never waits till they arrive at her nest, but boldly runs to meet them: when she has come as near them as she dares venture, she then rises with a loud screaming before them, seeming as if she were just flushed from hatching; while she is then probably a hundred yards from the nest. Thus she flies, with great clamour and anxiety, whining and screaming round the invaders, striking at them with her wings, and fluttering as if she were wounded. To add to this deceit, she appears still more clamorous, as more remote from the nest. If she sees them very near, she then seems to be quite unconcerned, and her cries cease, while her terrors are really augmenting. If there be dogs, she flies heavily at a little distance before them, as if maimed; still vociferous and still bold, but never offering to move towards the quarter where her treasure is deposited. The dog pursues, in hopes every moment of seizing the parent, and by this means actually loses the young; for the cunning bird, when she has thus drawn him off to a proper distance, then puts forth her powers, and leaves her astonished pursuer to gaze at the rapidity of her flight. The eggs of all these birds are highly valued by the luxurious; they are boiled hard, and thus served up, without any further preparation.

If we regard the figure of the Toad, there seems nothing in it that should disgust more than that of a frog. Its form and proportions are nearly the same; and it chiefly differs in colour, which is blacker; and its slow and heavy motion, which exhibits nothing of the agility of the frog; yet such is the force of habit, begun in early prejudice, that those who consider the one as an harmless, playful animal, turn from the other with horror and disgust. The frog is considered as a useful assistant, in ridding our grounds of vermin; the toad, as a secret enemy, that only wants an opportunity to infect us with its venom.

The imagination, in this manner biassed by its terrors, paints out the toad in the most hideous colouring, and cloaths it in more than natural deformity. Its body is broad; its back flat, covered with a dusky, pimpled hide; the belly is large and swagging; the pace laboured and crawling; its retreat gloomy and filthy; and its whole appearance calculated to excite disgust and horror: yet upon my first seeing a toad, none of all these deformities in the least affected me with sensations of loathing: born, as I was, in a country where there are no toads, I had prepared my imagination for some dreadful object; but there seemed nothing to me more alarming in the sight, than in that of a common frog; and indeed, for some time, I mistook and handled the one for the other. When first informed of my mistake, I very well remember my sensations: I wondered how I had escaped with safety, after handling and dissecting a toad, which I had mistaken for a frog. I then began to lay in a fund of horror against the whole tribe, which, though convinced they are harmless, I shall never get rid of. My first imaginations were too strong not only for my reason, but for the conviction of my senses.

144

To Mrs Bunbury

[London, c. December 25, 1773]

Madam.

I read your letter with all that allowance which critical candour would require, but after all find so much to object to, and so much to raise my indignation, that I cannot help giving it a serious reply. I am not so ignorant madam as not to see there are many sarcasms contain'd in it, and solœcisms also (solœcism is a word that comes from the town of Soleis in Attica among the Greeks, built by Solon, and applied as we use the word kidderminster for curtains from a town also of that name, but this learning you have no taste for) I say madam there are sarcasms in it and solœcisms also. But not to seem an ill-natured critic Ill take leave to quote your own words and give you my remarks upon them as they occur. You begin as follows,

> I hope my good Doctor you soon will be here
> And your spring velvet coat very smart will appear
> To open our ball the first day in the year.

Pray madam where did you ever find the Epithet good applied to the title of Doctor? Had you calld me learned Doctor, or grave Doctor, or Noble Doctor it might be allowable because these belong to the profession. But not to cavil at triffles; you talk of my spring velvet coat and advise me to wear it the first day in the year, that is in the middle of winter. A spring velvet in the middle of winter?!! That would be a solœcism indeed. And yet to encrease the inconsistence, in another part of your letter you call me a beau. Now on one side or other you must be wrong. If Im a beau I can never think of wearing a spring velvet in winter, and if I be not a beau – why – then – that explains itself. But let me go on to your next two strange lines

> And bring with you a wig that is modish and gay
> To dance with the girls that are makers of hay.

The absurdity of making hay at Christmass you yourself seem

145

sensible of. You say your sister will laugh, and so indeed she well may – the lattins have an expression for a contemptuous kind of laughter, *naso contemnere adunco* that is to laugh with a crooked nose, she may laugh at you in the manner of the ancients if she thinks fit. But now I come to the most extraordinary of all extraordinary propositions which is to take your and your sister's advice in playing at Loo. The presumption of the offer raises my indignation beyond the bounds of prose it inspires me at once with verse and resentment. I take advice! And from who? You shall hear.

> First let me suppose what may shortly be true
> The company set, and the word to be Loo.
> All smirking, and pleasant, and big with adventure
> And ogling the stake which is fixd in the center.
> Round and round go the cards while I inwardly damn
> At never once finding a visit from Pam.
> I lay down my stake, apparently cool,
> While the harpies about me all pocket the pool.
> I fret in my gizzard, yet cautious and sly
> I wish all my friends may be bolder than I.
> Yet still they sit snugg, not a creature will aim
> By losing their money to venture at fame.
> Tis in vain that at niggardly caution I scold
> Tis in vain that I flatter the brave and the bold
> All play in their own way, and think me an ass.
> What does Mrs Bunbury? I sir? I pass.
> Pray what does Miss Horneck? Take courage. Come do.
> Who I! Let me see sir. Why I must pass too.
> Mr Bunbury frets, and I fret like the devil
> To see them so cowardly lucky and civil.
> Yet still I sit snugg and continue to sigh on
> Till made by my losses as bold as a lion
> I venture at all, while my avarice regards
> The whole pool as my own. Come give me five cards.
> Well done cry the ladies. Ah Doctor that's good.
> The pool's very rich. Ah. The Doctor is lood.

Thus foild in my courage, on all sides perplext,
I ask for advice from the lady that's next
Pray mam be so good as to give your advice
Dont you think the best way is venture fort twice.
I advise cries the lady to try it I own.
Ah! The Doctor is Lood. Come Doctor, put down.
Thus playing and playing I still grow more eager
And so bold and so bold, Im at last a bold beggar.
Now ladies I ask if law matters youre skilld in
Whether crimes such as yours should not come before Fielding
For giving advice that is not worth a straw
May well be call'd picking of pockets in law
And picking of pockets with which I now charge ye
Is by Quinto Elizabeth death without Clergy.
What justice when both to the Old Baily brought
By the gods Ill enjoy it, tho' 'tis but in thought.
Both are placed at the bar with all proper decorum.
With bunches of Fennel and nosegays before em.
Both cover their faces with mobbs and all that
But the judge bids them angrily take off their hat.
When uncovered a buzz of enquiry runs round
Pray what are their crimes? They've been pilfering found.
But pray who have they pilfered? A Doctor I hear.
What, yon solemn fac'd odd looking man that stands near,
The same. What a pitty. How does it surprize one
Two handsomer culprits I never set eyes on.
Then their friends all come round me with cringing and leering
To melt me to pitty, and soften my swearing.
First Sir Charles advances, with phrases well strung
Consider Dear Doctor the girls are but young.
The younger the worse I return him again.
It shews that their habits are all dy'd in grain.
But then theyre so handsome, one's bosom it grieves.
What signifies handsome when people are thieves.
But where is your justice; their cases are hard.
What signifies justice; I want the reward. –

147

Theres the parish of Edmonton offers forty pound; there's the parish of St Leonard Shoreditch offers forty pound; there's the parish of Tyburn from the hog in the pound to St Giles's watch house offers forty pound, I shall have all that if I convict them.

> But consider their case, It may yet be your own
> And see how they kneel; is your heart made of stone?
> This moves, so at last I agree to relent
> For ten pounds in hand, and ten pound to be spent.
> The judge takes the hint, having seen what we drive at
> And lets them both off with correction in private.

I chalenge you all to answer this. I tell you you cannot. It cuts deep. But now for the rest of the letter, and next – but I want room – so I believe I shall battle the rest out at Barton some day next week. I dont value you all.

Afterword: Goldsmith and Politics

There are certain writers whom it has always seemed easy to label, and Goldsmith is one of them. My own reading and re-reading of his work, however, has led me to feel that the labels are wrong, or are stuck on in the wrong places. Thackeray's label, 'the most beloved of English writers', is especially adhesive. Yet there are at least two major objections to it. In the first place it threatens to sentimentalize work which, though it may possess a surface charm and accommodating sweetness of manner, on closer inspection frequently turns out to be full of hidden snags. It is, for example, customary to tag *The Vicar of Wakefield* 'a charming comedy'. But as Seamus Deane has remarked, the novel has an ironic, subversive intent which is 'consistently undermining the theme of the Vicar's inexhaustible benevolence'.[1] I would go further than this and say that although benevolence may look to be Goldsmith's characteristic solution to certain problems, it invariably ends up being the problem itself, a fact of which he is by no means unaware. In the second place, Thackeray begs the question. In what sense can you call a writer 'English' who was born and grew up in rural Ireland and who spent some formative years at Trinity College, Dublin?

Yeats, it is true, thought that Goldsmith had forfeited his Irishness, that by choosing to write as he did he had 'come to seem part of the English system'. But later he changed his mind, and very damagingly described Goldsmith as a type of the Irishman who is 'the gentle, harmless – you might call it saintly – type, that knows no wrong, and goes through life happy and untroubled, without any evil or sadness.'[2] This is to damn with faint praise. Yeats's revised version presents Goldsmith as Dr Primrose. It is to ignore the 'Man in Black', that *alter ego* as John Ginger has rightly identified it, who operates as a 'reminder of tragic possibilities beneath the bustling activities and the gaudy clothes.'[3] And anyway, what of *The Deserted Village*? *That* poem knows no wrong?

And yet it would be silly to deny that Yeats was right to detect

149

in Goldsmith a readiness to play the part of a certain type of Irishman. The 'English' man of letters, familiar friend of Samuel Johnson and the Club, of Sir Joshua Reynolds and his circle, of Lord Clare and social grandees like the Bunburys – this Goldsmith seems to have been only too ready to adopt a role with which he and they could feel safe. (There is presumably a barb lurking in Henry James's praise for the 'amenity' of Goldsmith's style – all things to all men.) He could not or would not rid himself of his Irish brogue, nor of an 'affected silliness' which Reynolds put down to his desire to 'lessen himself', i.e. make himself not feared nor envied, but liked. And underneath this 'sensitive amiability'[4] there was a self-destructive streak which Johnson recognized, Boswell condescended to, and others wrote off as rash imprudence rather than the self-hatred which it may well have been. Playing at being 'English', playing the 'stage Irishman': either way Goldsmith ends up as a tame, 'beloved' writer, not out to cause anyone any trouble, evading the implications of his own subjects, 'adorning everything he touches' (the words are from Johnson's epitaph), drenching his material in a golden haze of pastoral simplicities.

There is a measure of truth in this version of Goldsmith. Seamus Deane has been particularly critical of the evasiveness. He takes issue with what he calls Goldsmith's

> most unconvincing attack upon 'Luxury'. This is Goldsmith's half-hearted way of dealing with the ever-renewable dispute between metropolitan and provincial life, between, say the Lissoy of his youth and the Vauxhall he patronised in his maturity. In Ireland, the contrast between the world of fashionable Dublin and the rest of the country was especially painful. If Luxury were the cause of it, then Luxury was only another name for colonialism of the most rapacious kind. But, like the rest of his Irish friends, Goldsmith could not quite see Ireland as a colony of England. It had to be, in some fashion, incorporated into English civilisation, an integral part of it...In effect, Goldsmith's account of the passage from provincial pastoralism to

urban frivolity and materialism is futile, because it amounts to little more than an amateur attempt to explain away the Irish-English tension which is at the heart of his experience.[5]

This is subtle and at the same time hard, a good deal harder than those like John Montague, who argue that if *The Deserted Village* is in the end unfocused, this is not so much because Goldsmith is trying to explain anything away, as because he is trying to explain too much. Auburn cannot be both Lissoy *and* an English village, much as Goldsmith may try to affect a synthesis of the two.

Donald Davie takes a position different from either Deane or Montague, although agreeing with both that there is something unsatisfactory about Goldsmith's most famous poem. He therefore chooses to direct attention towards *The Traveller*, because in this poem, he argues, we can see Goldsmith's political and social credo set out with absolute clarity. It is that of the Tory monarchist, very much within 'the English system'.

> ...*The Deserted Village* prescribes no remedy for the state of affairs it deplores, and therefore puts no reader under obligation to do anything about it. *The Traveller* however *does* prescribe a remedy: enhanced power for George III.... *The Traveller* is a fervent apologia for the monarchical form of government, taking the time-honoured ground that, since the underprivileged need a power to appeal to above the power of local privilege, the only such power conceivable is the power of the Monarch, elevated above all sectional interests.[6]

The lines from the poem to which Davie refers in making his case include such key moments as those where Goldsmith speaks about 'contending chiefs' who 'blockade the throne, / Contracting regal power to stretch their own,' as a result of which he asks his brother to 'curse with me that baleful hour, / When first ambition struck at regal power.' Such moments undoubtedly show Goldsmith in the role of Tory monarchist and there is any amount of evidence that he played the part with some consistency. Boswell records him saying as late as 1773, 'I'm for the Monarchy to keep us equal',[7] and in his *History of England* he notes ruefully of the 1760s that 'The strength of the crown was every day declining, while an aristocracy filled up every avenue to the throne, intent only on emoluments, not the duties of office.'[8] It is this aristocracy, composed of the 'contending chiefs', which for the most part can be brought together under the familiar title of the Whig Supremacy, against which Goldsmith inveighs. His opposition to these people is plain enough, as well as being constant. And it therefore follows that his Tory monarchism is a deep-rooted and unshakeable conviction.

Or does it? Suppose we put the lines to which Davie refers into context. Goldsmith says that he has been watching with 'Fear, pity, justice, indignation,' the chiefs at their work; and he continues:

> 'Till half a patriot, half a coward grown,
> I fly from petty tyrants to the throne.
>   Yes, brother, curse with me that baleful hour,
> When first ambition struck at regal power;
> And thus polluting honour in its source,
> Gave wealth to sway the mind with double force.
> Have we not seen, round Britain's peopled shore,
> Her useful sons exchanged for useless ore?
> Seen all her triumphs but destruction haste,
> Like flaring tapers brightening as they waste;
> Seen opulence, her grandeur to maintain,
> Lead stern depopulation in her train,
> And over fields where scattered hamlets rose,
> In barren solitary pomp repose?
> Have we not seen at pleasure's lordly call,
> The smiling long-frequented village fall:
> Beheld the duteous son, the sire decayed,
> The modest matron and the blushing maid,
> Forced from their homes, a melancholy train,
> To traverse climes beyond the western main....

Here, of course, we have the seed from which *The Deserted Village* will later flower, although Donald Davie and others think the latter poem a deformed growth, because it is calculated not to give offence, is too guarded, too bland. By the same token they maintain that the vigour of *The Traveller* depends on Goldsmith's readiness to argue that greater power for George III would have prevented the newly enriched aristocracy from furthering their selfish ambitions by enclosing land for their parks and country houses and, in the process, abusing what should have been their social and political responsibilities.

I am not convinced. Of course, Goldsmith attacks the largely Whig aristocracy. But can we be so sure that his poem champions George? 'And thus polluting honour in its source.' Why should we not read this line as implying that the king is part of the problem? I think not only that we can, but that we must; to justify this I need to go back to the first version of *The Traveller*, called 'A Prospect of Society'. The history of the writing and publication of this draft of *The Traveller* is extremely complicated (although it has been meticulously unravelled by Roger Lonsdale). It is enough for my present purposes to note that in this earlier text, when Goldsmith speaks of seeing 'contention hem the throne', he feels that

> I can't forbear: but, half a coward grown,
> I wish to shrink from tyrants to the throne.
>   Yes, my lov'd brother, cursed be that hour
> When first ambition toil'd for foreign power;
> When Britons learnt to swell beyond their shore,
> And barter useful men for useless ore....
> Have we not seen, at pleasure's lordly call,
> An hundred villages in ruin fall?

The passage attacks the Whig aristocracy and looks to monarchy to champion the dispossessed. But when it reappears, revised and expanded, in *The Traveller*, matters are not nearly so straightforward. For one thing, the original 'half a coward' has now been joined by 'half a patriot', and this is bound to be highly problematic given the way that Goldsmith has used the word 'patriot' earlier in the poem. (I leave out of account a reference at line 357 to 'patriot flame', since this identifies a past when patriotism could be simple, as it cannot now.) In lines 73-4 he remarks: 'Such is the patriot's boast, where'er we roam, / His first, best country ever is at home.' And a little later: 'Though patriots flatter, still shall wisdom find / An equal portion dealt to all mankind.' In other words patriots suffer, as patriots will, from a blinkered, irrational pride in their own country. Goldsmith would have met many of them in London. When he comes to speak of himself as 'half a patriot' I do not for a moment believe that he would have forgotten the loaded way in which he had already used the term. Nor would he have expected his readers to have forgotten. The point then is that he is wryly admitting to having almost fallen into the patriotic trap, while retaining enough wit to recognize that it *is* a trap. And this recognition, we must surely reflect, comes more readily to a writer who balances uneasily between two national identities. A paraphrase of Goldsmith's meaning might then run something like this: 'Here I am, having half deluded myself into trying to believe that one big tyrant is better than many small tyrants.' For – and this is the second significant alteration – the original 'tyrants' have now become 'petty tyrants', presumably to contrast with George III, who then becomes the biggest tyrant of them all. Goldsmith would not have been alone in thinking of George in this way. As J.H. Plumb remarks: 'Powers that [George] had every right to exercise seemed despotic when employed by him. It is not remarkable that the grotesque myth that he was aiming at tyranny should have been so widely believed so early in his reign....'[9]

Davie might argue that although Goldsmith may well have regarded George as a tyrant, it was as an essentially benevolent one, so that we are to view the king, through the poet's eyes at least, as the Good Natured Man and the Vicar of Wakefield rolled into one. And as we shall see, Dr Primrose does indeed speak out in favour of the one big tyrant, although in less than flattering terms. But that does not solve the problem about Goldsmith's reference to honour as polluted in its source which, it should be

154

noticed, is the third crucial way in which the text of *The Traveller* is different from 'A Prospect'. For in that earlier version, Goldsmith had accused ambition of toiling for foreign power, and we know where we are with this, can have no doubt at whom the finger is being pointed: at East and West Indian traders and all those who were bent on prolonging hostilities against France. What we have then to explain is why Goldsmith changed the lines, why, no matter how slyly, he gives the impression that you have to be a bit of a fool – half a patriot – to believe that the monarchy can offer a way out of the mess the country is in, especially since this particular monarch is himself infected by what's rotten in the state.

The short answer to this question is that Goldsmith is probably having fun at the expense of his English friends, and adroitly covers his tracks so that Johnson, say, could not openly accuse him of anti-monarchical or anti-English bias (which for Johnson amounted to the same thing). More seriously, Goldsmith is, I think, properly exploiting his double vision, the vision of an Anglo-Irish writer, in order to open up questions about the kind of patriotism that is rooted in Tory monarchism. Most seriously of all, and involving the longest answer, Goldsmith is attempting to come to terms with 'Old Corruption': that is, the state of England as he saw it, which aroused in him a mixture of disquiet and contempt, even though this had occasionally to be hidden under the surface of, and could be compromised by, his role as 'beloved English writer'.

In 1762 Goldsmith published in *Lloyds Evening Post* a short essay called 'The Revolution in Low Life'. The essay, which has frequently been referred to as '*The Deserted Village* in prose', tells how the writer had spent the previous summer in 'a little village', which he recalls as an ideally 'happy community'. But: 'I was informed that a Merchant of immense fortune in London, who had lately purchased the estate on which they lived, intended to lay the whole out as a seat of pleasure for himself'. As a result the community was to be destroyed. 'All the connexions of kindred were now irreparably broken; their neat gardens and well

155

cultivated fields were left to desolation.' The tale ends with Goldsmith generalising from his experience: 'I am informed that nothing is at present more common than such realities.' As a result, 'wherever the traveller turns, while he sees one part of the inhabitants of the country becoming immensely rich, he sees the other growing miserably poor....' The ultimate cause of this revolution in low life is foreign commerce, which makes governments at length 'Aristocratical; and the immense property, thus necessarily acquired by some, has swallowed up the liberties of all. Venice, Genoa, and Holland, are little better at present than retreats for tyrants and prisons for slaves.'

Seamus Deane refers to this conclusion in order to take exception to it. 'Inaccurate or irrelevant' he calls Goldsmith's examples, and adds, 'Ireland, after all, would have prospered a great deal more had the restrictions on its trade been lifted.'[10] I can agree to this while feeling that Deane is being less than fair to Goldsmith. For these three examples turn up again in chapter 19 of the *Vicar of Wakefield* (most of which was almost certainly written in 1762), and here we learn from Dr Primrose that in Holland, Genoa and Venice, 'the laws govern the poor, and the rich govern the law.' What does that remind us of? Those lines in *The Traveller* where Goldsmith claims that 'Each wanton judge new penal statutes draw, / Laws grind the poor and rich men rule the law.' And here he is talking about England. Thus if Deane is right to argue that Goldsmith could have focused his case more appropriately by drawing attention to the exploitation of Ireland by the English, it can also be said that by stitching together a number of apparently disparate moments, we are able to see how consistently Goldsmith argued against 'Aristocratical' government in England, even though he may not always make the argument explicit. He is unswervingly hostile to the influence of those whom Plumb terms the 'West Indians, the East Indians, the bankers, the brewers', as well as the 'thickening strata of the professional classes' and the 'new industrialists'.[11] In short, he is at odds with all those 'who believed by instinct that England was destined to great wealth if only her opportunities were not scotched by the incompetence of her King and his ministers'; and these newly influential people inevitably included among their ranks members of the Irish nobility, 'gorged with recent plunder . . . buying their way into the English aristocracy'.[12] Goldsmith knew what these people had done to the country he had grown up in, and he would have had little time for their natural spokesman, Pitt, who protested vehemently against the Preliminaries of the Peace of Paris. In Pitt, Plumb remarks, 'the voice of the City spoke. His denunciations were based entirely on commercial strategy.'[13]

Goldsmith's angry contempt for the 'Merchant of immense fortune' is, then, entirely proper and is implicitly on behalf of the dispossessed of Ireland as much as it is explicitly on behalf of those of England. And this will help to explain why he uses monarchical government as a stick with which to beat the aristocracy. Thus, no doubt, Dr Primrose's diatribe against tyrants.

> Now, Sir, for my own part, as I naturally hate the face of a tyrant, the further off he is removed from me, the better pleased I am. The generality of mankind are of my way of thinking, and have unanimously created one king, whose election at once diminishes the number of tyrants. (*The Vicar of Wakefield*, ch. IV)

Donald Davie refers to this speech by way of making his case, and he insists that Primrose's position is not finally different from Goldsmith's. But to speak of hating the face of a tyrant is hardly an enthusiastic endorsement of George III. And anyway, can we so easily identify Primrose with his creator? Yes, both are against the aristocracy. Yes, both see in the monarchy a preferable alternative. But there are things Goldsmith knows that Primrose does not know, or which at all events he chooses not to know; and it is these which make a commitment to monarchism problematic. They include the fact that benevolence may well turn out to equal impotence – as it does for Honeywood and Primrose. More importantly, however, they include the knowledge that it is not easy to dissociate the one big tyrant from the many petty ones. To see why this is so we need to turn yet again to the village.

157

It is 'distant about fifty miles from town, consisting of near an hundred cottages'. This is the village as discussed in the 'Revolution in Low Life', and it is not very specific. But then nor are the accounts of the 'little neighbourhood' to which Dr Primrose retreats (though this borrows some of its details from the other), nor the 'smiling, long-frequented village' of *The Traveller*. And Auburn may seem more a generalized picture than one derived from a real place. Nevertheless, the work of Mavis Batey has made it virtually certain that the village Goldsmith in all cases had in mind was Nuneham Courtenay, in Oxfordshire, which is indeed about 'fifty miles from town'. Between 1760 and 1761 Lord Harcourt began the process of 'improving' his land there. This required the destruction of a church and a village. Parsonage, ale-house, cottages and long-established gardens were wiped out and the duck-pond was expanded into a lake. The village was removed to the main road some mile and a half away, and new cottages were put up on either side of the road there.[14] Only one villager remained behind and we know about her because she is the subject of a poem by William Whitehead. Some time in the 1760s Whitehead wrote an 'Inscription for a Tree: On the Terrace, at Nuneham, Oxfordshire'. A note to the poem tells us that

> This tree is well-known to the country people by the name of BAB's tree. It was planted by one BARBARA WYAT, who was so much attached to it, that, on the removal of the village of Nuneham, to where it is now built, she earnestly intreated that she might still remain in her old habitation. Her request was complied with, and her cottage not pulled down till after her death.[15]

Whitehead treads carefully. On the one hand he wants to pay tribute to the woman who might well be called – and who almost certainly was – 'the sad historian of the pensive plain'. On the other, he needs to avoid giving offence. He had been Harcourt's tutor and was still close to him.

But there is perhaps another reason for Whitehead's caution, which is that as Poet Laureate he would have to avoid giving offence to the king, and that included avoiding criticisms of those close to the king. And Harcourt was particularly close to him. In 1750 he had been appointed governor to the future George III, at that time Prince of Wales.[16] Ten years later he acted as an important functionary at George's coronation. The following year he was appointed special ambassador to Mecklenburg-Strelitz, in order to negotiate George's marriage with the princess Elizabeth, whom he accompanied back to England. After the wedding Harcourt became master to the queen's horse, an appointment which, so the *Dictionary of National Biography* informs us, he relinquished on being made 'lord chamberlain of the queen's household'. And all this time he was at work on the 'improvement' of Nuneham Courtenay. In his study of *Georgian Gardens*, David Jacques claims, on what evidence I do not know, that Harcourt was 'famous for his republican leanings'.[17] If so, they must have emerged after the period with which I am concerned, or, more likely, Jacques is confusing Harcourt with his son, who continued his father's improving work. At all events, Goldsmith would have been only too aware that this intimate of the king was responsible for the wanton destruction of a village, and that he was thus an example of cumbrous pomp pitted against the peasantry's interests. Small wonder, then, that Goldsmith should find it impossible to make a simple or even workable opposition between king and aristocracy. I shall return to this point, but first, some further evidence that will help to dislodge the conventional view of Goldsmith as an unquestioning Tory monarchist – for that is the view that lies behind Thackeray's praise, just as it lies behind the regular and easy accommodation of Goldsmith as a quintessentially English writer.[18]

On 23 April 1763, John Wilkes published his famous attack on the king, in no.45 of the *North Briton*. As a result, he was arrested on a charge of seditious libel, and at once became a hero for many and a villain for some. Among the latter was Samuel Martin, Secretary to the Treasury and one of Bute's creatures, who challenged Wilkes to a duel and badly wounded the 'champion of

Liberty'. Wilkes's cause was taken up by Charles Churchill, in a poem called *The Duellist*, which hailed liberty as felt, enjoyed and adored 'far beyond the reach of Kings'. Churchill was already notorious for his attack on the acting profession in *The Rosciad* (1761), a poem the question of whose authorship had let Smollett, one of Goldsmith's mentors, into an undignified squabble with Churchill and his Whig friends. Here, then, was a perfect opportunity for Goldsmith to speak out for *his* friends and on behalf of the values of Toryism and throne. Yet he remained silent. John Ginger is at a loss to know why. Goldsmith 'seemed to have deliberately let slip the chance to add to his income by entering the battle... under the command of Smollett.' But to put it this way opens up disturbing implications. Ginger is therefore quick to reassure us. Goldsmith's 'political views were none the less strong and consistent. He was a committed monarchist...'[19] If so, one can only reflect that he had an odd way of showing it. Goldsmith might well have thought that though Wilkes took his stand on Liberty, events had proved there was not much in it for him. It was of course a contemporary commonplace that England was the land of the free. Foreign observers were quick to contrast the state of affairs in England with their own, repressive regimes. England is 'passionately fond of liberty', Montesquieu noted in 1729, 'every individual is independent.'[20] Goldsmith for one thought such independence 'prized too high'. He coined that phrase for *The Traveller*, with the 'contending chiefs' in mind. But he could hardly have applied it to Wilkes, at least not without an uneasy awareness that the law which was being visited on the champion of Liberty was the same law which promoted Harcourt's interests, and that Harcourt was an intimate of the king whom Wilkes had attacked – very mildly, too, be it noted.

After his wounding Wilkes fled to France, where he stayed some four years. But by 1768 he was back in London and again in trouble. His election as MP for Middlesex led to his immediate arrest and temporary release, 'until such time as a writ of *capias ut legatum* had been served against him'. A week later it was. The riots provoked by the law's treatment of Wilkes culminated in what became known as the Massacre of St George's Fields, when at least eleven people were killed by the Foot Guards who had been called up to disperse Wilkes's supporters. Moreover, on the evening of his temporary release from custody, Irish coal-heavers, who had been involved in a strike for higher wages, appeared on the streets of London in a show of support for Wilkes, and as a result of the ensuing violence seven of them 'were sentenced to death at the Old Bailey and hanged at the Sun Tavern Fields in Stepney before a crowd of 50,000, attended by three hundred soldiers and 'a prodigious number of peace officers'.[21]

In *Oliver Goldsmith: His Life and Works*, A. Lytton Sells notes that sometime at the end of the 1760s Goldsmith was approached by a Dr Scott, who tried to hire him to write on behalf of the North government, which was being 'hard-pressed by the opposition in Parliament and by Junius, Wilkes and . . . other political writers.' Goldsmith was apparently 'so absurd as to say – *'I can earn as much as will supply my wants without writing for any party; the assistance therefore you offer, is unnecessary to me,'* and so I left him . . . in his garret.'[22] It goes without saying that Goldsmith was rarely in funds; at various times he earned a great deal of money, which was usually spent at a prodigious rate. Sells can make neither head nor tail of it. Goldsmith would 'have performed a public service by writing in support of the ministry.' In addition, we are assured that Goldsmith disliked Wilkes, and in 1773 'actually wrote in support of James Townsend who had put up against Wilkes for election as Lord Mayor of London. Other men of distinction supported North's ministry, including Johnson who had published three pamphlets in its favour.'[23] Sells is therefore left as baffled as Ginger by this odd failure of Goldsmith's amenability.

But consider the public service that Goldsmith would have apparently performed if he had written for North and against Wilkes. Seven coal-heavers, Irish at that, had been hanged for rioting as part of a demand for better wages, other people had been cut down by a hail of army bullets. All were supporters of

Wilkes. 'The laws govern the poor, and the rich men govern the law.' Horace Walpole noted with smug satisfaction that Goldsmith 'meddled not with politics', a claim which Donald Davie rightly rejects in his account of *The Traveller*. My point is that by attending not merely to what Goldsmith says, but to what he does not say, we can get a better sense of his political thinking. In choosing not to meddle with the politics of party when they are directed against Wilkes, Goldsmith is being political. Look at Goldsmith from the vantage point of the Tory monarchist, and his behaviour is a puzzle. Look at him from the vantage point that best illuminates *The Traveller* and his silence makes sense. It is at once wily and stubborn. He is not going to be jockeyed into a position that will make him a tame 'English' writer.

There is another point. North was George's Prime Minister and his trusted confidant. In *The Great Arch: English State Formation as Cultural Revolution*, Philip Corrigan and Derek Sayer remark that they are not the first 'to observe that property ("owning, being owned") and propriety ("correctness of behaviour or morals") have the same etymological root. State activities were central to the naturalisation of both.'[24] And the principal means of attaining that naturalisation was the Law. How far Goldsmith was alert to this we can note if we pause on a couplet which at first may seem remote from such considerations.

> Along the lawn, where scattered hamlets rose,
> Unwieldy wealth and cumbrous pomp repose.

The contrasts are pregnant with implications. Goldsmith presents the hamlets as natural growths: not so much fashioned in an 'orderly' or 'formal' way as vigorously flourishing because 'scattered'. The term offers a rebuke to Capability Brown's concept of how to make a landscape look natural, which insistently required a 'scattering' of trees. For Goldsmith, it is human activity which in its purposefulness is truly natural, *not* the mimic art of the landscape architect; and it contrasts with all that is 'unwieldy' and 'cumbrous' – words which point up the uselessness – inutility – of wealth and pomp. For whatever is unwieldy obviously cannot

162

be handled, and as for cumbrous, Johnson's various definitions are greatly to the point: 'Troubling; vexatious; disturbing', 'oppressive; burthensome', 'jumbled; obstructing each other'. The word thus plays back with a bitter irony on orthodox connections between property and propriety. What could be less proper than that the land be cumbered by these useless heaps of wealth? Yet pomp monopolizes 'the real benefits of nature' as Goldsmith notes elsewhere.[25] And it is enabled to do so because 'rich men rule the law'.

Goldsmith snaps the argument shut when, later in *The Deserted Village*, he re-introduces pomp.

> Here, while the proud their long-drawn pomps display,
> There the black gibbet glooms beside the way.

At first glance the couplet may seem to provide a violent disjunction. But we are then bound to recognize the causal interconnectedness between the two displays. After all, very little in eighteenth-century life was attended with greater pomp than the law. As E.P. Thompson in particular has pointed out, law's theatrical, ritualized qualities were a way of insisting that the Law was above the law.[26] Enactment of the law therefore developed as a spectacle, and we have seen that one such spectacle was attended by an audience of 50,000. This may seem far removed from another aspect of the eighteenth-century: 'The much remarked "civilized" tone of . . . upper-class life – fenced-off parks, elegant mansions with their classical façades and formal gardens . . .'[27] That it is not is crucial to Goldsmith's repeated use of the word 'pomp', attached at one point to emparked land, at another to the streets of London where the gibbet glooms, and prompting the reflection that cultural treasures 'have an origin which [the cultural materialist] cannot contemplate without horror. They owe their existence not only to the efforts of the great minds and talents who have created them, but also to the anonymous toil of their contemporaries. There is no document of civilization which is not at the same time a document of barbarism.'[28] You do not have to claim Goldsmith as a cultural materialist in order

163

to realize that Walter Benjamin's famous words apply to much of the material presented in *The Deserted Village*.

This then leads to the all-important question: what exactly is Goldsmith's attitude to the material he presents? It plainly cannot be pinned down by the word 'horror'. Disquiet? Yes, sometimes. Despair? Yes, again. Nostalgic condescension – a way of belittling the importance of his own subject? Yes, yet again. What this amounts to is the admission that there may well be something finally evasive about the tone of *The Deserted Village*, and it was probably this that Raymond Williams had in mind when he remarked that as soon as Goldsmith's feelings for his villagers 'is extended to memory and imagination... what takes over... is a different pressure: the social history of the writer.'[29] As we have seen, that social history is a complex matter and it exposes Goldsmith to contradictions that the very nature of his subject is bound to exacerbate, and which he may try to evade by that attack on 'luxury' which Deane finds so inaccurate. John Montague puts the case more forgivingly, perhaps, when he speaks of Goldsmith's 'skilful alternation between images of original innocence and malignant destruction',[30] and John Barrell takes this further by suggesting that the most radical element in the poem is Goldsmith's appeal, not so much on behalf of the industrious poor, as on behalf of leisure: his interest is in the periods 'when toil remitting lent its turn to play':

> But this concentration on leisure may have been precisely the point, a point confirmed by that feature of the village before its destruction which, in the description which opens the poem, is most conspicuous by its absence – the hall. For the bold peasantry of England, thought Goldsmith, the lightest labour would easily secure the necessities of life, if as freeholders once again they were obliged neither to pay rent, nor to work for money wages. Goldsmith disengaged the labourer from his 'proper' and 'natural' identity as a labourer, as a man born to toil, and suggested that he could be as free to dispose of his time as other poets agreed only the rich man or the shepherd was free to do.[31]

Barrell's argument has much to recommend it, and from my point of view it is especially useful because of the way in which it enables us to see that the Adamic 'soft primitive' state of leisure Goldsmith invokes can hardly be consonant with that more feudalistic vision which, be it never so 'innocent', is part and parcel of the fervent and uncomplicated Tory monarchism Davie wishes onto him, and which certainly depends on the presence of the Hall, to whose absence from the pre-deserted village Barrell rightly draws attention. (Whereas such a Hall, together with its estate, is part of the habitation to which the Vicar of Wakefield retreats; and that this in no way clouds Dr Primrose's golden view of society is one reason among many why it will hardly do to identify him with Goldsmith.) To say this is not to deny the passion of Goldsmith's attack on Whig wealth and pomp. These matters provide him with his 'vision of decay consequent upon imperial expansion and excessive trade', and they make for some of the poem's greatest moments.

> Kingdoms by thee to sickly greatness grown,
> Boast of a florid vigour not their own.
> At every draught more large and large they grow,
> A bloated mass of rank unwieldy woe;
> Till sapped their strength and every part unsound,
> Down, down they sink, and spread a ruin round.

In these mordant lines England becomes both a Rowlandson-like parody of gluttonous excess and a grotesque vision of overblown fruitfulness, a garden whose original, Adamic 'florid vigour' has turned into an over-run park. The wit is formidable, the lines packed with vivid awareness of how this wealth-congested England has become a weed-infested 'unwieldy' chaos. (The word comes into play again with stunning effect.) This is the fruit of the private, competitive spirit, unforgettably laid bare.

The passage may also seem at first to bring comfort for all those wishing to claim Goldsmith as that true patriot, the Tory monarchist. For there is no difficulty in identifying the Whig sympathies of most of the new men of wealth, nor in listing their

165

acquisitions of land and property. Among them you will find the very grandest, Pitt, Earl of Chatham, and Robert, Lord Clive. Moreover, both employed Brown to carry out improvements on their land, Chatham in 1765, Clive in 1769; and what this entailed has been often enough spelt out by historians of landscape architecture, who have had to note that the great scale of Brown's gardens could not have been achieved without the help of enclosure acts. No wonder, then, that the host of improvers should earn Goldsmith's scorn. By contrast, he was free to admire Shenstone's garden at Leasowe's because it was on a small scale, reared with no man's ruin, no man's groan. (Except, that is, Shenstone's: he spent so much on it that it ruined him and his heirs had to sell it off in order to settle the debts he left.)

But it won't do. I have already remarked on the fact that at the time Harcourt began his work of improvement he was an intimate of the king. And this one example can be almost endlessly multiplied, so that even if we choose to resist the identification of Auburn with Nuneham Courtenay, we would have finally to admit that 'improvement' was by no means left to Whig aristocrats, even though this has been argued by those who wish to free themselves from the complications of historical circumstance. It may be for this reason that they forget to number Bute among the improvers. Yet when George's first Prime Minister and most trusted ally left office in 1763, he set about landscaping his properties at Luton Hoo and Highcliffe; and he appointed Brown to plan and supervise the work. Goldsmith would have known about that, just as he would have known about George's appointing Brown in 1764 to be Royal Surveyor of Gardens and Waters. If we seek an explanation of why the text of 'A Prospect of Society' was re-written for *The Traveller* this will do as well as any. Of course it is true that Brown was especially friendly with leading Whigs. He was bound to be. They had a great deal of money and were bent on acquiring land. They therefore guaranteed him important commissions. But he had no objection to being friendly with Tories and they had no objection to being friendly with him, and it is nonsense to pretend otherwise. Luxury, pomp, Law: these constituents of Old Corruption are not simply a function of any one party, and if Goldsmith began by thinking or hoping that this was the case, he was bound to become disillusioned; and the disillusionment would grow the more he travelled around England, as he did during the 1760s. It is this swelling disillusionment and the occasional struggle to contain or suppress it which accounts for the contradictions discoverable in most of his work, and above all in *The Deserted Village*.

For on the one hand we have a poem which is recognisably Augustan in its nostalgic placing of 'The swain mistrustless of his smutted face', and all too clearly the work of an amenable poet, one who knows on which side his bread is buttered. He was after all a professional man-of-letters in eighteenth-century London, and it is the professional who is to the fore when it comes to the presentation of village life in terms of a lost idyll. Davie presumably has this aspect of the poem in mind when he says that it prescribes 'no remedy for the state of affairs it deplores'. How could it? The pastoral poem as picturesque exercise rests on the assumption that loss, however regrettable, is also inevitable. It comes about through a 'principle of change.'[32] Regret or sadness can then be easily indulged, the more easily the more the idyll is placed in the past. Besides, which of Goldsmith's readers would wish to be a smutty-faced swain or, for that matter, to share the Vicar of Wakefield's retreat, or be part of the happy community described in the 'Revolution in Low Life'? 'They were merry at Christmas and mournful in Lent, got drunk on St George's-day, and religiously cracked nuts on Michaelmas-eve.' This way of writing is a way of writing down and therefore writing off. It allows for – indeed, it ensures – an evasion of proper interest in its own subject. It assuages where it should hurt. You can find such writing in *The Deserted Village*, and for some readers at least this fatally compromises the poem's worth.

Yet in the dedication to Reynolds – 'all my views and enquiries have led me to believe those miseries real, which I here attempt to display' – and elsewhere in the poem there is, as we have seen, an insistence on identifying the causes of the state of affairs

167

Goldsmith deplores; and these have nothing to do with the so-called 'principle of change'. On the contrary, they are social actualities. Not to acknowledge this element, nor the force it has in the poem, is to refuse to see the troubled, radical wit that takes Goldsmith well beyond an amateur indictment of luxury as the root of the village's – and England's – evils, and which leads him to a formidably suggestive account of how luxury, or more accurately Pomp, operates through and by means of specific social agencies. Here there is no room for evasion and none for compromise. At the heart of the matter is Law, functioning in the name of the Crown. And in more than name. For it is not Whig aristocrats alone who profit from the connection of Law with Pomp. The monarchy, George III and his cronies, are an integral part of Old Corruption. 'In England,' Tom Paine wrote two years after Goldsmith's death, 'a king hath little more to do than to make war and to give away places; which in plain terms, is to impoverish the nation and set it together by the ears.' I do not suggest that Goldsmith would have assented to the truth of Paine's words. I do suggest, however, that Paine could have looked to elements in *The Deserted Village* to vindicate them. In the end it is Goldsmith's recognition of the deep-seated and widespread power of Law and Pomp, uncertain and compromised though this recognition may sometimes be, makes him a far more valuable writer than can be suggested by the term 'beloved'. For that is blandly coercive. It promises to absorb Goldsmith into a version of Englishness from which he tried to distance himself, and from which we should want to detach him.

Notes

'A Prologue': This imitation first appeared in *An Enquiry into the Present State of Polite Learning*, 1759. Decimus Liberius (106-43 BC) was a 'Roman knight famous for his poetical talents in writing pantomimes'. Goldsmith's own note remarks that Caesar forced Liberius upon the stage and that this piece, 'written with great elegance and spirit... shews what opinion the Romans in general entertained of the profession of an actor.'

'On a Beautiful Youth...': First printed in *The Bee*, no i, 1759. [See p.177] Goldsmith says that it was imitated from the Spanish, but it is entirely possible that the epigram is an original work: it is typical of a kind popular throughout the eighteenth century.

'The Gift': First printed in *The Bee*, no ii, 1759: an imitation 'Etrène à Iris' by Bernard de la Monnoye, in *Ménagiana*, a collection of which Goldsmith was to make further use.

'A Sonnet': First printed in *The Bee*, iii, 1759, in imitation of a poem by Denis Sanguin de Saint-Pavin.

'An Elegy on... Mrs Mary Blaize': First printed in *The Bee*, no. iv and modelled on a kind of poem which appears in *Ménagiana*. Lonsdale notes that Kent-Street was a well-known haunt of beggars.

'The Double Transformation': First printed in the *Weekly Magazine* in 1760, although it may have been written much earlier. The subject is a familiar one in eighteenth-century poems, especially Swift ('Strephon and Chloe') and Pope (Clarissa's speech in *The Rape of the Lock*). Goldsmith's octosyllabics are lighter than Swift's, and his tone a good deal less savage.

169

'Description of an Author's Bed-chamber': First printed in a 'Chinese Letter' in the *Public Ledger*, 1760 and subsequently published in the *Citizen of the World*, 1762. [See p.177] Some of the details were importantly taken over into *The Deserted Village*. Lonsdale is almost certainly right to say that the poem has 'a strong autobiographical content', and it is probably picked up in chapter X of *An Enquiry* (see below p.176). But the subject was a familiar one: Hogarth's *The Distrest Poet* (1737) was widely known, and literary London was aware of the sad life and death of the poet Samuel Boyse. He had been befriended and helped by Samuel Johnson, but, according to one account, was found dead in bed of starvation, pen in hand, in 1749.

'On Seeing Mrs *** ...': First printed in a 'Chinese Letter', 1760, with a prefatory note in which Goldsmith explains that he is parodying the kind of 'stage poet' who watches 'the appearance of every new player at his own house, and so come[s] out next day with a flaunting copy of newspaper verses.'

'On the Death...': First printed in a 'Chinese Letter', 1761. Again modelled on the kind of poem to be found in *Ménagiana*.

'An Elegy on...a Mad Dog': First printed in *The Vicar of Wakefield*, 1766, although Lonsdale thinks it may have been written in 1760, when 'London was seized with something of a panic about mad-dog bites'. Model to be found in *Ménagiana*.

'Stanzas on Woman': First printed in *The Vicar of Wakefield*, although possibly written some years earlier. *The Vicar* was probably written by 1762.

'Edwin and Angelina': This ballad, sometimes called 'The Hermit', was printed in *The Vicar*. There were at first mutterings that Goldsmith had plagiarised Percy's ballad 'The Friar of

Orders Grey', which appeared in his famous *Reliques of Ancient English Poetry*, 1765, but Percy himself pointed out that Goldsmith's ballad had been written earlier – the two men were friends – and suggested that both of them owed something to another ballad, 'Gentle Heardsman'. Leaving this aside, what matters is Goldsmith's recognition of the significance of the newly-discovered ballad tradition. * This stanza was first printed in 1801.

'Songs':   Two songs from *The Captivity: an Oratorio*, completed by 31 October 1764. Lonsdale says that there was something of a vogue for oratorios that year. Goldsmith's libretto is deeply undistinguished, although the two songs deserve to survive. I print the 1776 versions, which I assume Goldsmith to have revised with an eye to independent publication. He wrote another similar hack work, *Threnodia Augustalis* in 1772.

'The Traveller':   This poem was probably a long time in the making. It first appeared at the end of 1764 but may have been begun as early as 1755, when Goldsmith was on the Continent. Lonsdale's interesting account of the poem's genesis and development may be supplemented by Pat Roger's essay in *The Art of Oliver Goldsmith*, ed. A. Swarbrick (1984). Lines 429-34 and 437-8 are by Johnson.
Luke and George Zeck were engaged in a rebellion in Hungary against the Turks, as a result of which George was condemned to sit on a red-hot throne, wearing a red-hot crown and holding a red-hot sceptre. Robert-François Damiens attempted to assassinate Louis XV, was horribly tortured, and then torn to pieces by wild horses.

'A New Simile':   First printed in 1765. Lonsdale points out that Goldsmith's model was in fact Thomas Sheridan's 'A New Simile for the Ladies', which was printed with Swift's reply to it in editions of Swift's *Works* after 1738. Andrew Tooke's *The Pantheon, Representing the Fabulous Histories of the Heathen Gods and Most Illustrious Heroes* was 'a popular schoolbook...illustrated with copper-plates, including that referred to throughout this poem', (Lonsdale, p.658).

'Verses in Reply...': This verse impromptu was written on 20 January 1767. Dr George Baker was physician to Sir Joshua Reynolds, and the persons referred to in the verses were part of the Reynolds circle. Mrs Hannah Horneck was Reynolds' Devonian friend; 'The Jessamy Bride' was her elder daughter, Mary (Partridge says jessamy is a corruption of *jessamine* or *jasmin* and means fashionable, even dandified); little Comedy was her younger daughter, Catharine; the Captain in Lace her fifteen-year old son, Charles. Mrs Nesbitt was a sister of Henry Thrale, Johnson's friend, and Angelica Kauffman was a famous eighteenth-century painter who, together with Reynolds, had been the subject of adulatory verses in the *Advertiser*.

'Epitaph on Edward Purdon': Edward Purdon had been a fellow-student of Goldsmith's at Trinity College. A makeshift career concluded with a forlorn attempt to earn a living in London as a professional writer. He died in great poverty on 27 March 1767.

'Epilogue': *The Good-Natured Man* was first performed at Covent Garden on 29 January 1768. The Royal College of Physicians was in Warwick Lane, and the 'brother Doctor' is almost certainly George Baker.

'Epilogue': Written in February 1768 for Charlotte Lennox's *The Sister*, which found little favour when it was first performed, although Goldsmith's skilful piece of jobbing was exempted from the general criticism.

172

The Deserted Village: Goldsmith's great poem was written between 1768-70; the last four lines were contributed by Johnson. The poem is dedicated to Reynolds and the following passage from the Dedication is of obvious importance:
> I know you will object (and indeed several of our best and wisest friends concur in the opinion) that the depopulation it deplores is no where to be seen, and the disorders it laments are only to be found in the poet's imagination. To this I can scarce make any other answer than that I sincerely believe what I have written; that I have taken all possible pains, in my country excursions, for these four or five years past, to be certain of what I allege; and that all my views and enquiries have led me to believe those miseries real, which I here attempt to display.... In regretting the depopulation of the country, I inveigh against the increase of our luxuries; and here also I expect the shout of modern politicians against me. For twenty or thirty years past, it has been the fashion to consider luxury as one of the greatest national advantages; and all the wisdom of antiquity in that particular, as erroneous. Still however, I must remain a professed ancient on that head, and continue to think those luxuries prejudicial to states, by which so many vices are introduced, and so many kingdoms have been undone.

The subject had indeed pre-occupied Goldsmith since 1762 at the very least, in which year he published 'The Revolution in Low Life'. (see below p.178). 'Altama' (line 344) is a river in Georgia, USA: 'Torno' and 'Pambamarca' (line 415) refer to a Swedish river and town on the Gulf of Bothnia, and a mountain in Ecuador.

'Epitaph on Dr Parnell': In 1770, Goldsmith wrote a *Life* of Thomas Parnell (1679-1718), for an edition of his poems published that year. If the epitaph was intended for the edition it failed to appear there, and its first printing was posthumous with 'The Haunch of Venison', in 1776.

'The Haunch of Venison':   Lonsdale suggests that the poem was written between late 1770 and the beginning of 1771. Robert Nugent (1702-88) became Viscount Clare in 1766. He had been an MP since 1741, and was Vice-Treasurer for Ireland 1760-5 and 1768-82, as well as President of the Board of Trade. Goldsmith seems to have become friendly with this influential and wealthy man in the latter half of the 1760s; although his poem is in some ways an imitation of Swift and Boileau, it is marked by that easy familiarity of manner which goes some way towards explaining Henry James's recommendation of the 'amenity' of Goldsmith's style. 'A bounce' (line 14) is a boastful lie. 'Mr Burn' (line 18) was Michael Byrne, Clare's nephew. The Monroe referred to in line 24 is Dorothy Monroe (1709-1803), a celebrated beauty of the day. Lonsdale suggests that the list of names in line 27 must be those of impoverished writers, of whom the only one identifiable with certainty is Paul Hiffernan (1719-77). The quotation in line 60 is from a letter from Henry, Duke of Cumberland, to Lady Grosvenor, which was produced as evidence at his trial for adultery with her, in July 1770 (Lonsdale, p.700). For Clare see J. Ginger, *The Notable Man* (1977) pp.214-16.

'Prologue to *Zobeide*':   Joseph Cradock's play was first performed at Covent Garden on 11 December 1771. Goldsmith seems to have become friendly with the wealthy Cradock at about this time.

'Song':   This song was preserved by James Boswell, who published it in the *London Magazine* in June 1774. According to Boswell, 'it was intended to be sung by Miss *Hardcastle* . . . . but it was left out, as Mrs Bulkeley who played the part did not sing. He sung it himself in private companies very agreeably.

The tune is a pretty Irish air, called *The Humours of Balamagairy*, to which, he told me, he found it very difficult to adapt words; but he has succeeded admirably in these few lines.'

'Epilogue': Goldsmith made no fewer than three attempts to write a satisfactory epilogue for his play, and although all three have survived, I have chosen to print only the one used for the play's first production, in March 1773. The Nancy Dawson referred to in line 26 was a dancer at Sadler's Wells who became especially famous in 1759, for her dancing of the hornpipe in the *Beggar's Opera*. *'Che faro'* is a reference to an aria in Gluck's opera *Orfeo*. 'Heinel' (line 28) refers to Anna-Frederica Heinel, another famous dancer of the day. (Lonsdale, pp.724, 729.)

'Epilogue': Written in Spring 1773 for Charles Lee Lewes (1740-1803), the original Young Marlow in *She Stoops to Conquer*, better known as a pantomime Harlequin. Ginger says that until he played Marlow, 'he had never been trusted with a speaking part of any significance' (p.317).

'Retaliation': Begun early in 1774 and left unfinished at Gold-smith's death on 4th April. It was started as a riposte to those friends of the club who had agreed among themselves to write mock epitaphs on his death. Garrick seems to have been in the forefront of those who dreamed up the idea, and immediately produced his 'Impromptu': 'Here lies NOLLY Goldsmith, for shortness call'd Noll, / Who wrote like an angel, but talk'd like poor Poll.' There is an edge in this – Garrick was probably not best pleased at having been proved wrong in his low estimation of *She Stoops to Conquer* and his reluctance to mount the play – and Goldsmith's retaliation is even more barbed. Because the poem is so full of local references I have decided to follow in this instance the textual notes and practice of Charles Cowden Clarke, in Gilfillan's edition (1863). The notes are thus at the

175

foot of the relevant page. The Dr Dodd referred to in line 86 was a popular preacher, as well-known for the scandals surrounding his name as for his professed piety. He was eventually hanged in 1777. 'Be-Rosciused' in line 118 refers to the famous Roman comic actor, Roscius, and, by implication, to Charles Churchill's *The Rosciad*, 1761, a satire on the acting profession.

PROSE

[On Ovid's *Epistles*]:   This wittily destructive essay, which probably owes something to Pope's earlier devastating attack in the *Guardian* on Philips' *Pastorals*, shows Goldsmith both in Grub Street, writing for a living, and at the same time displaying a critical acumen that is anything but the product of mere hack work.

An Enquiry...:   Goldsmith's first book was published in April 1759. These extracts give the flavour of his literary and social concerns, especially – and crucially – as he reflects on the developing gap between worth and wealth. Not surprisingly, this was a widely-shared preoccupation among eighteenth-century writers who wanted to be professional, who distrusted patronage, and yet were required to drudge for their daily bread.
p.87   Jerome-David Gaubius (1705-80), the 'chymicall Professor' at Leyden.
p.89   'Etiam victis...' from the *Aeneid*, 2.367: 'Even the conquered take fresh heart, and the conquerors fall.'
p.91   'Sale, Savage...'   George Sale (1697-1736), Orientalist and translator of the Koran. Richard Savage, a talented scribbler, who died in poverty in 1743, was guaranteed posthumous

fame when Johnson became his biographer. Nicholas Amherst
(1677-1747), poet and essayist. Edward Moore (1712-57), dram-
atist. The *Persian Eclogues* were the work of the poet William
Collins, who, at the time Goldsmith was writing, was known
to have sunk into a state of melancholy madness.

p.92 'Sint Moecenates...' from Martial, *Epigrams*, 8.56.5:
'Grant us patrons like Maecenas, Flaccus, and there will be no
lack of Virgils.'

p.96 'Civem mehercule...' from Cicero, *Epistulae ad Familiares*,
ii.4.1: 'On my oath, I don't think there is a citizen in existence
who can laugh these days.'

From *The Bee*: Goldsmith planned to issue *The Bee* as a weekly
paper, beginning in October 1759. It died after eight issues,
and when printed in book form at the end of the year was
coolly received. For all that, it contains some of Goldsmith's
most alert critical and discursive writing.

p.102 'Toga quae...' from Horace's *Satires*, 1.3.14-15: 'And
a cloak, however coarse, to keep out the cold.'

p.102 'Minus juvat...' adapted from Pliny's *Letters* 4.12.7:
'A widespread reputation is of less value than a great one.'

p.106 'Nam qua...' from Ovid, 'I scarcely claim as mine what
I have not achieved myself'.

p.108 'a most whimsical figure' John Hill M.D. (1716?-1775).
A journalistic quack and famous eccentric, of whom Garrick
wrote: 'For farces and physics his equal there scarce is: / His
farces are physic, his physic a farce is.'

p.109 'The person who came after him...' Arthur Murphy
(1727-1805), dramatist.

p.110 'another whose appearance...' David Hume (1711-76).
His *Natural History of Religion* appeared in 1757.

p.111 'a person that seemed more inclined...' Tobias Smollett
(1721-71), for whose *British Magazine* Goldsmith was soon to
write, which no doubt explains the measure of flattery.

The Citizen of the World: comprised letters which had first appeared in the *Public Ledger*, from shortly after its inception in January 1760 until August 1761; published in 1762. The idea was by no means original. Montesquieu's *Lettres Persanes* (1721) had sparked off a vogue for tales in which 'oriental' travellers reported back to their fellow-countrymen on the absurdities and corruptions of European countries. (For a good account, see Seamus Deane's essay on *The Citizen* in Swarbrick, op. cit.)

'The Revolution in Low Life':   This brief essay, which appeared in *Lloyd's Evening Post* in June 1762, was established as indubitably the work of Goldsmith by R.S. Crane in 1922. Its important relationship to *The Deserted Village* is now widely recognized. p.135 'Strata jacent...' is a combination of Virgil, *Eclogues* vii.54 – 'strata jacent passim sua quaeque sub arbora poma' (everywhere the fruit lies under its parent tree) – and *Georgics* i.118: 'nec tamen, haec cum sint hominumque boumque labores' (nor yet, though toiling men and oxen have thus laboured). Goldsmith is deliberately fusing passages which speak of toil, fruitfulness, the possibility of future difficulties, and sterility of the soil.

An History of the Earth...:   Goldsmith contracted to supply this work in 1765, but it dragged on for years and was completed only just before his death. Commentators have noted that very little of it is original, and Goldsmith's taxonomy is orthodox in its Augustan acceptance of a chain of being, which is everywhere implicit in his work.

'To Mrs Bunbury':   Lonsdale extracts the verses and treats them as a separate poem, but I think the letter deserves to be read as a whole. Catherine Horneck Bunbury, the 'Little Comedy' of 'Verses in Reply to an Invitation to Dinner at Dr Baker's', had written to Goldsmith inviting him to spend New Year 1774 at the family seat at Great Barton, Suffolk. 'Pam' is the knave of clubs, higher than the knave of trumps.

2   W.B. Yeats, *Uncollected Prose*, eds Frayne and Johnson, Macmillan, 1975, p.403.
3   J. Ginger: *The Notable Man: The Life and Times of Oliver Goldsmith*, Hamish Hamilton, 1977, p.362.
4   Quoted by B. Harris, 'Goldsmith in the Theatre', in *The Art of Oliver Goldsmith*, ed. A. Swarbrick, Vision Press, 1984, p.150.
5   Deane, op. cit. pp.126-7.
6   Donald Davie, 'Notes on Goldsmith's Politics', in Swarbrick, op. cit. pp.83-4.
7   Quoted by Roger Lonsdale in *Gray, Collins and Goldsmith*, Longmans, 1969, p.653.
8   Ibid.
9   J.H. Plumb, *The First Four Georges*, Fontana edn., 1966, pp.123-4.
10 Deane, op. cit. p.126.
11 Plumb, op. cit. p.103.
12 J.H. Plumb, *England in the Eighteenth Century*, Penguin, 1950, p.182.
13 Plumb, *The First Four Georges*, p.104.
14 Mavis Batey, 'Oliver Goldsmith: An Indictment of Landscape Gardening', in *Furor Hortensis*, ed. P. Willis, Elysium Press, Edinburgh, 1974.
15 William Whitehead, *Plays and Poems*, two vols, H. Dodsley, London, 1774, vol.2, p.234.
16 It seems that the following year he resigned over a quarrel with the Prince's tutors who, he claimed, were too much in favour of Absolutism. Perhaps this is the origin of David Jacques' belief that Harcourt had republican leanings.
17 David Jacques, *Georgian Gardens: The Reign of Nature*, Batsford, 1983, p.94.
18 More than one commentator has noted that in 'The Description of an Author's Bed-chamber' Goldsmith speaks of his possessing a print of 'The twelve good rules'. These rules were said to have been discovered in Charles I's room after his execution and if you believe that the author's bed-chamber is based

being fervent monarchists has not done the villagers much good, especially since their plight has been caused by the king's friend: in this light, the lines inevitably become ironic.

[19] J. Ginger, op. cit. p.162.

[20] Quoted in Roy Porter, *English Society in the Eighteenth Century*, Penguin, 1982, p.271.

[21] For all this see George Rudé, *Wilkes and Liberty*, Oxford, 1962, pp.45-97 passim.

[22] A. Lytton Sells, *Oliver Goldsmith: His Life and Works*, Allen & Unwin, 1974, pp.132-3.

[23] Ibid. p.135.

[24] P. Corrigan & D. Sayer, *The Great Arch: English State Formation as Cultural Revolution*, Blackwell, 1985, p.96.

[25] See the essay on 'The Poor Man's Cow' p.137.

[26] See especially *Whigs and Hunters*, Penguin, 1975, although this insight is one to which Thompson repeatedly returns in his work.

[27] Corrigan and Sayer, op. cit. p.102.

[28] Walter Benjamin, *Illuminations*, Fontana edn, 1973, p.258.

[29] Raymond Williams, *The Country and the City*, Chatto and Windus, 1973, p.78.

[30] J. Montague, 'The Sentimental Prophecy: A Study of *The Deserted Village*', in Swarbrick, op. cit. p.96.

[31] J. Barrell, *The Dark Side of Landscape*, Cambridge, 1980, p.78.

[32] The de-mystifying of the picturesque is an important part of much recent writing about the eighteenth-century. Barrell's book is a most valuable contribution to the work, as is Williams's *The Country and the City*. My own essay 'Wordsworth and the anti-Picturesque' (in J. Lucas, *From Romantic to Modern Literature*, Harvester, 1982) tries to tease out further strands.